Autistic children

Special needs in education

SERIES EDITOR
Ron Gulliford, Professor of Education
University of Birmingham

Autistic children
Teaching, community and research approaches

compiled and edited by

Barbara Furneaux

and

Brian Roberts

with contributions from
Sybil Elgar
Jeanne Hertzog
Les Scarth
Jill Boucher

Routledge & Kegan Paul
London, Henley and Boston

First published in 1977
by Routledge & Kegan Paul Ltd
39 Store Street,
London WC1E 7DD,
Broadway House,
Newtown Road,
Henley-on-Thames,
Oxon RG9 1EN and
9 Park Street,
Boston, Mass. 02108, USA
Set in Compugraphic Baskerville
and printed in Great Britain by
Ebenezer Baylis and Son Ltd
The Trinity Press, Worcester, and London

British Library Cataloguing in Publication Data

Autistic children – (Special needs in education).
1. Autism   2. Mentally handicapped children –
Education
I. Furneaux, Barbara II. Roberts, Brian III. Series
371.9'2   LC4580   77-30239

ISBN 0 7100 8704 7

This book is dedicated to Dr Mildred Creak—a pioneer in this difficult field—whose advice and encouragement we wish to acknowledge in this way.

Contents

Series editor's preface   *page* ix

Foreword by Mildred Creak   xi

Contributors   xiii

Authors' note   xiv

1 Introduction   1
   BRIAN ROBERTS

2 Description of the condition of autism, and theories
   of causation   21
   BRIAN ROBERTS

3 Differential diagnosis   43
   BARBARA FURNEAUX

4 The teacher, the parents and the environment   57
   BARBARA FURNEAUX AND BRIAN ROBERTS

5 Working with the younger children   91
   BARBARA FURNEAUX

6 Further education and training for the autistic
   adolescent   121
   SYBIL ELGAR

7 Research and the teaching of autistic children   140
   JILL BOUCHER AND LES SCARTH

CONTENTS

8 The specialist advisory services   162
   JEANNE HERTZOG

9 Summary and discussion   182
   BARBARA FURNEAUX AND BRIAN ROBERTS

Series editor's preface

This series of books on special educational needs will be concerned with the practice of special and remedial education whether in ordinary or special schools, with the findings and implications of research and with the discussion of organisation and provision. The series aims to provide informed accounts of the needs of different groups of handicapped pupils and how these needs may be met by appropriate teaching, therapy and care.

These aims are well exemplified in this book which provides an account of the present state of our understanding of the puzzling condition of autism as well as an account, based on intensive experience of teaching and caring for autistic children and young people, of what can be done by teachers in the school, by parents in the home and by the community through the co-ordination of specialist services and by the organisation of special provisions. In the case of most handicapping conditions we have a fairly clear idea of what is needed to minimise the handicap, even if we do not always organise special help as effectively as we would like. In the case of autistic children we are both uncertain of the nature of the condition and its treatment and, perhaps because of this, only slowly developing special provisions.' Nevertheless, as the contributors to this book show, much can be done and more could be done.

I know that the authors of this book hope that it will contribute to a more widespread and informed knowledge of the problems of diagnosing autism, of the findings of research, of the positive steps that can be taken to help autistic children and their families and that it will help to stimulate the development of special schooling and care.

Foreword

This book is primarily a handbook for teachers and for those helping in schools or classes provided for autistic children. Interest in this particular problem has widened very much in the last twenty years but it has done so without medical and allied researches reaching the core of the problem, namely any precise cause for autism. The very fact that the patterns of behaviour so often seen in autistic children are so characteristic tempts us to suppose that one day one factor will emerge which explains everything. This looks likely to remain an unfulfilled dream for a long time to come.

We are, however, because of the background research and clinical observation now available, much clearer as to what is needed in the way of help for these children. A valuable feature in this book is that no single pattern of practical help is laid down, and no one reading it can fail to realise that immense frustrations will face anyone involved in working with autistic children. This is well seen in chapters 7 and 8, where the multiple facets needing investigation are shown to involve an unusually wide range of consultants. In all such detailed work, whatever the specialist may contribute from his own field, we emerge knowing that there is still left facing us the need to meet such a handicapped child's everyday requirements. In many ways, parents at home and teachers in the school will have the longest as well as the hardest job to do.

So here is a book written from a background of handling such everyday experiences. I am glad that it has been written from this standpoint if only because, in a vague and unsolved problem, it is dangerously easy to refer it all to 'someone who knows' the answer. It is made very clear here, first, that no one knows the answer, and second, that while waiting for it we have the reality situation pressing upon us every time we meet such a child. Clearly this falls most heavily on those who live with them, and those who seek to help them educationally day by day.

Most importantly we are shown that here education is not a problem of learning so much as primarily a problem of opening up communication. How can we begin to communicate with a child whose doors are not open, who shows little curiosity, and no rapport with new people and the demands of daily life?

As time goes on attention is more and more focused on this aspect of autism. It is indeed the very core of the problem, since no child can become part of a civilised society, much less earn his living, make his contribution and enjoy doing so, without some means of communicating with others.

As this book makes clear, non-communication has a two-way thrust, and for a harassed parent nothing is easier than to put an autistic child in a safe place from which he can't escape, and leave him to it. And then, how non-communicating can they (parents and siblings) become towards their autistic child?

Perhaps the most encouraging thing about the book as a whole is that while it covers a wide field, looking at the challenge from various aspects, it offers a continuing and creative approach, but no solution, to what we all must recognise as an on-going problem. Those who work in this field should find it an encouraging book to read.

MILDRED CREAK, MD, FRCP, DPM
Hon. Fellow Royal College of Psychiatry
Hon. Physician to Hospital for Sick
Children, Great Ormond Street

Contributors

Dr Jill Boucher, Research Assistant, Charles Burns Clinic, Birmingham.

Sybil Elgar MBE, Principal, Somerset Court, Brent Knoll.

Barbara Furneaux, Principal, The Linden Bridge School, Epsom.

Dr Jeanne Hertzog, Consultant Child Psychiatrist.

Brian Roberts, Educational Psychologist and Honorary Lecturer, Faculty of Education, University of Birmingham.

Dr Les Scarth, Consultant-in-Charge, Charles Burns Clinic, Birmingham.

Authors' note

All the views and opinions expressed in this book are the author's own and do not necessarily reflect in any way those of their several employers or University Departments, nor do they necessarily coincide with those of the other contributors.

The editors and publishers would like to thank the following for permission to reproduce copyright material: Leo Kanner for the Appendix to chapter 2; the National Society for Autistic Children for the list of nine points on pp. 25–31; Professor Michael Rutter and the *British Journal of Psychiatry* for a quotation from his article.

1 Introduction

BRIAN ROBERTS

Prologue

Timothy was 4 when I met him. His mother was a part-time teacher and had contacted me as the educational psychologist in the area about one of the children she taught; she did not mention her son on that occasion. While visiting a pre-school playgroup some time later, Timothy was brought to my notice by the playgroup leader because he did not speak to anyone, was always on his own and did not appear to understand the world about him. He would sit on the floor for much of the day picking up a brick and dropping it. When I approached him, his head lowered over the brick-dropping task as if he were more intensely interested in it. When I raised his head and put his face between my hands to achieve eye contact with him he focused on a spot at the middle of my forehead; as I moved my head upwards to get him to look into my eyes, he lifted his gaze higher to my forehead again.

His mother, when I saw her, conceded that he was somewhat unusual; she said Timothy had developed normally until the beginning of his third year and then stopped speaking. As he was now due to start school she was worried that he might not manage the reception year very easily. However, she thought he was improving, and her husband, also a teacher, considered Timothy to be fairly normal.

I told her I thought it might be the case that Timothy was autistic and if so he was far from normal, and would need a considerable amount of treatment to attain anything like normal behaviour.

I then spent some time enquiring about possibilities for obtaining treatment for him in the area, but nothing that seemed appropriate either in hospitals or special education units was available. His mother clung to the hope that he would be all right in school, but there he lasted only three weeks, during which time his behaviour, which included having apparently unstimulated attacks of rage, screaming and kicking at anything, became too difficult for the teacher to handle. He was also a very fast runner, and would disappear from the school, but stop somewhere nearby as he did not appear to know the way to his home, which was in fact quite near the school.

The local education authority supplied a teacher to see Timothy at home for a few hours each week. Because he did not speak (it had by now been confirmed that he was not deaf) and did not respond to anything she attempted with him, such as reading stories, playing games like 'clap-hands', 'insy-winsy spider', etc., she soon became dispirited in trying to make any connection with a child who was vastly different from any she had taught before.

As there was no other possibility for treatment I decided to see him once a week at a clinic, and these one-hour sessions lasted for six months. My room contained many things a child would love to play with, but nothing interested him. I tried all the things the home teacher had tried, and many other things also, to no avail. At the end of the six months there was still no speech, no appropriate behaviour, no interest shown in the surroundings. A social worker had been seeing mother at home, making suggestions as to what kind of things the parents might try with Timothy, but after strenuous efforts they seemed defeated and only just able to cope with their two younger children who were not abnormal. A psychiatrist who had seen Timothy at my request told the parents he also considered Timothy to be autistic and suggested to them that he should be educated in a training centre for severely subnormal children. They finally agreed to this and Timothy started there at the age of 5 years 8 months.

During the four years I remained in the area I went to see Timothy at the training centre about once a month. Over the first year his aggressive behaviour diminished; he became very placid and his teacher reported he stared into space for much of the time. He began to do jigsaws, even complicated ones, which he could complete at the first attempt. Sometimes he would fit the pieces together on the reverse side only, without the picture for cues; one jigsaw he completed, without any straight outside edges, took me twice the length of time to do. He also began to draw remarkably life-like faces with pencils and crayons though apparently he had not gone through the stage of drawing stick-figures. These drawings would have been remarkable for a talented 10-year-old. After a few months, however, he would scribble all over each drawing as soon as it was completed, and then he ceased drawing altogether; subsequently no inducement would get him to pick up pencil, crayon or paintbrush.

When I left the area in 1971 Timothy was 10 years old. The last time I saw him he was sitting at a table in the training centre staring through the window with unfocused gaze. When I again tried to look him in the eyes there was no change of focus. I felt he did not see me or perhaps even feel I had moved his face in my direction. The teacher reported that apart from the jigsaws which he still completed with unusual ease and speed there was nothing he tried to do. There was still no speech, and his parents wondered if he would be better off in a hospital for severely subnormal children, as they felt his presence at home disturbed their other children.

Many details have been left out of this illustration of an autistic child's non-entrance into the education system ten years ago. I had been interested in such children for a few years before I met Timothy, and knew that this sequence of events was by no means unusual. As an educational psychologist, there was little time I could give to him and when I did try to work with him I had virtually no useful ideas except those I had learned in treating other less abnormal children. Not one of these worked for Timothy. Other possibilities for treatment either in local day places or residential ones were, respectively, non-existent or of dubious relevance at that time.

Later the education authority were able to start a unit for such children which is now part of a school. As the reader will discover from this book, there is a possibility that Timothy's state might have been very different if he had been admitted to such a unit at the time I first saw him; on the other hand it might have remained much the same. It seems reasonably certain now, however, that with teaching-treatment at least some changes could have been made in his condition that would have benefited both him and his family.

Introduction

The teaching of autistic children has taken place in a structured way in England only in the last twenty years. By 'structured' is meant that a number of children labelled autistic have been provided with schools, classrooms or units with teachers employed to teach and treat them. (The question of using together the two terms 'teach' and 'treat' is dealt with later in the chapter.) It is true that some of the Rudolph Steiner schools have been dealing with autistic children for a much longer period than this. However, their teaching rationales and methods are .those deriving from the philosophy of education created by Steiner and in general are believed by Steinerians to be equally applicable to other forms of handicap, such as the different forms and conditions of severe subnormality. This book is mainly concerned first, with the specific techniques used when dealing with problems of learning and behaviour in autistic children and, second, with other issues which contribute to the treatment process.

Training of teachers

Training teachers specifically to work with autistic children has not yet materialised in England. There are courses of short duration, over a weekend or a few days, which are concerned with teaching issues among other aspects of autism, but in their nature and aims are not intended to give teachers an extensive training in dealing with these children. The National Society is at present exploring the possibility of a faculty or school of education at a British university initiating such a course, either as part of a diploma or degree in special education, or as a course in its own right. At the time of writing, no such course has yet begun. Thus this book is written in the hope that it will aid those teachers already interested in and/or teaching children with special educational needs, and specifically, autistic children. There is now a growing body of research about these children but little has been written on the everyday aspects of dealing with them and how they can be managed, taught and thus 'treated'.

Provision

There were three points of impetus in establishing separate provision for autistic children. The most telling perhaps was the creation of the National Society for Autistic Children, a registered charity formed in 1962 on the initiative of parents. Its first school was opened in Ealing, London, in 1965, 'as a pilot scheme to demonstrate the effectiveness of remedial education as a means to help children handicapped in this way and also to give training to teachers to be employed in future similar schools and classes' (NSAC pamphlet). Sybil Elgar was the first head of an NSAC school.

Preceding this, however, was Barbara Furneaux's unit at Hollymount, Wimbledon, which was opened in 1958 by Surrey County Council and which admitted two children labelled autistic in 1960 at the request of Dr Mildred Creak. The numbers of such children grew and in 1965 the school was moved, to become the Lindens School at St Ebba's Hospital in Epsom. By then admission was restricted to autistic and severely disturbed children. Sybil Elgar had also previously worked with individual autistic children, and there were some other school units beginning at this time, such as the one at Smith Hospital, Henley, and one at High Wick at St Albans, though generally in hospital units the children had been regarded as 'patients' rather than pupils until then.

A third major impetus was, more recently, the circular issued by the Department of Education and Science *Education of Autistic Children* (1971) requiring of each local education authority in England and Wales returns of numbers of diagnosed autistic children within the authority and statements of provision being made or planned for them. Until then it is perhaps correct to say that few education authorities had made special provision. Most autistic children were generally considered the responsibility of the Regional Hospital Boards and the Health Services, and so were mostly provided for either in the then Training Centres or in hospitals for the severely subnormal. The Lindens School was located in a hospital complex, but is financed and run by Surrey Education Committee. It moved to a purpose-built school outside the hospital in April 1977.

In April 1972 responsibility for training centres was taken over by education authorities, and in some areas this has led to the transfer of autistic children to special units.

Treatment

The term 'autistic children' was first used in 1943 by an American psychiatrist, Leo Kanner, who described a group of children who had not been classified as a distinct group previously. These children he claimed are distinct from those classifiable under the category of 'severely subnormal' and from others with unspecified forms of brain damage. Because the major characteristic, according to Kanner (see page 39 for the other Kanner criteria) was 'extreme aloneness', it was assumed in the USA that this feature could be treated by psychoanalytic techniques. Thus autistic children came to be treated in clinics and hospitals by child psychiatrists and psychotherapists. This still happens in both North America and Europe but such treatment is now much less common than formerly. A major problem with this kind of treatment has been the time available for the treatment programme which is, at best, usually an hour or two a week. An important factor where success has been demonstrated during these years has been the parents' ability to cope with the child during the periods between treatment. This would vary widely from family to family. Many parents, because of the severity of the child's problems, would scarcely be able to cope at all, especially if they also had other children.

As mentioned above, in 1971 in England local education authorities found they were now to be responsible for the education of autistic children. This must have come as a surprise to administrators, as the assumption had previously been held that such children needed specialised treatment *before* they could be educated. Many autistic children were considered to be adequately provided for in units and hospitals for severe subnormals. What Barbara Furneaux, Sybil Elgar and some others had demonstrated in the 1960s, however, was that the learning process for autistic children is (as it is for all children at a much earlier age) crucial to their general development and that the inter-communication process involved and developed in learning situations is indeed 'treatment', and is the salient factor because of the nature of these children's problems. Education and treatment are for them to some extent synonymous terms. This is implicit perhaps in the National Society for Autistic Children pamphlet's words 'effectiveness of remedial education as a means to help children handicapped in this way'.

Prognosis

It is probably reasonable to say that the problems involved in dealing with autistic children are more puzzling, varied and demanding than those of dealing with any other single category of handicap. Up to now the condition has proved the most intransigent of all to deal with. 'Success' in dealing with it is still, both in theory and practice, fraught with many conceptual difficulties. In view of the development of some children treated by Sybil Elgar and Barbara Furneaux it can now be seen that what may be aimed at is that the child who was autistic can, as an adult, cope with his life unaided in circumstances considered normal.

Nobody at the present time can predict the chances of improving the condition of any individual autistic child by the use of any teaching-treatment approach or any other method of treatment. Some children entering appropriate units and schools this year will possibly still be mute, apparently uncomprehending of the world they live in, and therefore likely to be totally unemployable, in twenty years' time. If provision then is similar to that of today, they will from their twenties onwards live permanently in the wards of subnormality hospitals. They will in general be infinitely less capable than some others occupying the same wards and as helpless as the most severely brain-damaged. On the other hand, despite the small increase in the amount of teaching/treatment resources in the last fifteen years, there is evidence that some children have improved beyond all expectation. As adolescents and young

adults they are at best unexceptional in the general population. This has happened at the National Society schools, the
Lindens School and a number of other establishments. These
children who began schooling in the severest autistic state have
made simultaneously (though not necessarily) excellent educational and social progress, to the point where they earn their
own living and in some cases manage their own lives. The
numbers are small in ratio to those who have not made such
progress. What is remarkable is that many of them have not
had 'treatment' as such, but have developed solely in an educational environment, either residential or day.

As mentioned earlier, one factor which may operate in this
development is the ability of the family to follow up the gains
made at school. Another is the age of starting education and
treatment, for the autistic child remaining in the severest state
is thereby deprived of the millions of social encounters and experiences available to the normal child and even to many
handicapped children from birth. The longer he remains in a
state where he is mute or echolalic, totally withdrawn or spasmodically aggressive, with no appropriate social behaviour,
having apparently neither the skill nor the desire to communicate, the larger the number of social encounters and stimulat-
ing learning experiences he misses out on.

As the teacher 'gets through' to the autistic child, much that
would have been learned spontaneously at an earlier age has to
be taught, and this may have to be done at first in the most
mechanical of ways. What would have taken place more or less
spontaneously between himself and his mother, his siblings
and playmates, now begins between himself and the teacher,
slowly, often painfully, and as a result of considerable skill and
patience on the part of those around him. Unlike the normal
baby he begins with no functioning communicating systems,
or at best extremely oblique and vague ones such as a temper
tantrum signalling a desire for food or evacuation. Such a
child may need many more years in which to develop skills
which did not emerge in the normal social and educational
processes. Even those who make good progress during primary
school years and can cope with secondary school may only
reach an adequate or good level of social maturity in their
twenties and thirties. It is therefore of great importance that

treatment begins at as early an age as diagnosis of the condition makes it clear and urgent need. As such a diagnosis is possible, perhaps, at around the age of 3 with many autistic children, it will be necessary for education authorities to consider making provision from that age. It may prove to be the case that the earlier the child is diagnosed and treated, the earlier he will be able to cope with normal education. Some of the pessimism which has been applied to the prognosis of the condition in the past may well be related to the lateness of the child's commencing treatment.

The label 'autism'

Another reason why prognosis has been pessimistic and perhaps why health and education authorities have seemed unwilling in general to invest in treatment and education is related to difficulties inherent in the label itself. Some general practitioners, psychiatrists, paediatricians and psychologists have maintained, since the Kanner descriptions, that autism is a term which describes a unique condition even if the combination of symptoms of the syndrome differs from child to child. Others have stated that so-called autistic children differ in their behaviour so much one from another, and the behaviour so overlaps that of other conditions that categorising children as autistic is virtually or totally useless. The main feeling of this latter group has appeared to be that it is pointless to expand provision further than is already provided for the various groups of 'subnormal' children.

It nevertheless seems now beyond dispute that some children who are extremely mentally and socially retarded even at the age of 5 and beyond show remarkable progress when treated by the methods described in this book. The manner in which they emerge from their isolation, begin to communicate and relate at first to adults and then to other children, and begin to learn to read and write and develop other cognitive skills, is quite distinctive when this group of children is compared with others grouped under the heading of 'mentally retarded'. The educational gains made by the latter usually proceed at a uniformly slow rate and are rarely dramatic, whereas typically the autistic child in his severest state shows no progress at all. As

9

he begins to make contact with others, however, the progress rate in educational terms is often far faster than that of a severely subnormal child. Some begin to make such progress while showing little or no improvement in communicating and social skills.

Other children diagnosed as autistic, even some of those obtaining apposite and skilled methods of treatment, have shown very little progress in any area. Perhaps this has been the most cogent argument against providing a postulated subgroup of severely subnormal children with relatively expensive treatment methods. Some of them remain totally alone and inert, passive or positively resistant to any attempt to 'reach' them. Other groups of severe subnormals, for example brain-damaged children and those with genetic defects, make relatively good progress. But, increasingly, autistic children receiving skilled help are making progress; the numbers of those making no progress is diminishing.

We do not yet know what the crucial influences are. Perhaps one such factor, as Barbara Furneaux shows in her chapter on differential diagnosis, is accurate distinction between children with different conditions who seem so similar at the time of initial diagnosis. Another may be the time of beginning treatment, and a third may be the family's ability to back up treatment received at school. Considering the enormous problems the child presents to the family, it is not difficult to imagine that much if not all the effective work done with the child in the treatment situation can be undone when he or she returns home in the evenings or during weekends and holiday periods. It may prove that these areas, singly or in combination, are significant in determining which autistic children progress and which do not.

Autistic children are diagnosed by their behaviour or, sometimes, lack of it. In their severest state they do not speak, or only echo what someone else has said, either immediately or after a period of time (delayed echolalia). If they move about (some will sit all day long motionless or producing one activity, such as lifting and dropping an object), they usually appear disinterested in their surroundings.

In fact, the behaviour of severely autistic children, unlike that of all except the most severely brain-damaged child, appears purposeless, but compares notably with that displayed by animals reared in strict isolation. Attempts to interest them in alternative behaviour are usually avoided or actively resisted, and can produce severe tantrums or attempts to escape the situation. They appear to have no sense of identity, and to inhabit an empty world. Bruno Bettelheim entitles one of his books about these children *The Empty Fortress*,[1] suggesting beleaguered psychological events, empty of thought or emotion, indifferent or resistant to any attempt at intrusion in their world. This is, of course, a speculation of what it is like to be an autistic child from the psychological standpoint. There is a fascinating published account by a young lady of what it was like to be autistic in Wing's book *Early Childhood Autism*.[2] The point is, we do not *know* what is going on 'in the child's head' during the time he remains autistic in his communication patterns, and even while he is achieving speech it is rare to hear even rudimentary references to himself, except in terms of needs.

The second, but perhaps central issue concerning the nature of the autistic condition, is that autistic children behave as if they cannot learn; in Gregory Bateson's phrase, they have not acquired the process of 'learning to learn' on repeated presentations of material attractive even to severely mentally retarded children (an instance might be brightly coloured formboards). Typically the autistic child initially appears puzzled or indifferent to the activities of others performing a learning task. He appears to have no motivation or ability to initiate or copy an activity. To overcome this negative position is the major concern of the teacher.

Prevalence of autism

Until 1964 no epidemiological studies of autism had been undertaken, and a paper written by J. K. Wing, N. O'Connor, and V. Lotter published in the *British Medical Journal*[3] says the prevalence then was unknown. This paper describes a survey begun in the then county of Middlesex in 1964 at the suggestion of the Medical Officer of Health.

The writers discuss the difficulty of identifying children said to be autistic. They took as their criteria 'Kanner's two

11

essential symptoms . . . in marked degree — that is, lack of responsiveness to people, and insistence on the preservation of sameness'.

These two criteria they used to identify the group which was termed the 'nuclear autistic group', i.e. those children who in their opinion revealed the most clearly defined attributes of autism. Two other groups were also identified: one termed a 'non-nuclear autistic group' who showed one or the other of the two Kanner criteria, but not both, plus 'other characteristics of the syndrome'; a third group was called 'non-autistic' and these children had 'only minor fragments of the syndrome'.

To select the children, a questionnaire was sent to teachers, school nurses, training centres (ESN schools), heads, and parents, of the population of Middlesex aged 8, 9 and 10. Nevertheless this may not be considered to be the 'total population', as children in hospitals for subnormals were not taken into account. The questionnaire was based on the Creak Committee's 'Nine Points' (see chapter 2), which includes both the Kanner symptoms noted above.

Fifty-four children were finally selected as falling into one of the three categories.

The breakdown of the groups is shown in Table 1.1.

Table 1.1

	Boys	Girls	Both sexes	Rate per 10,000
Nuclear autistic group	11	4	15	2·1
Non-nuclear autistic group	12	5	17	2·4
Total autistic children	23	9	32	4·5
Non-autistic group	13	9	22	—

Table 1.1 shows that, when the nuclear and non-nuclear groups are combined, the overall prevalence is 4·5 per 10,000 children of the age group 8 to 10. The authors comment that this is about twice the incidence of blind children in such a population; they also point to the fact of the excess of boys in all the groups and highest in the nuclear group (2·75:1).

From the information gathered about these thirty-two

autistic children, a number of interesting points emerge. A selection from these reveals:

(i) there was no evidence of likelihood for an autistic child to be first-born (which is a sometimes stated finding in other researches);

(ii) most of the autistic children had normal brothers and sisters;

(iii) three of them had abnormal EEGs (i.e. recordings of abnormal brain-waves, tending to suggest the possibility of defect in the brain); four had had convulsions;

(iv) the fathers of the nuclear autistic children were particularly likely to have occupations in the upper two social classes (out of five), which is a common finding in research on the parents of autistic children, but not always confirmed. A third of the fathers had had professional or university education.

Often it is argued in other researches that this finding is probably due to the fact that educated parents are likely to seek advice about their children more efficiently and refuse to accept a diagnosis of mental subnormality. However, on scrutiny of the data, the writers of this paper found nothing to suggest this was the case.

Thus the likely number of autistic children (if the incidence has not changed over the last ten years) between the ages of 5 and 14 is said by the authors to be about 3,000 in England and Wales (1,400 nuclear 1,600 non-nuclear). However, if it is considered that the condition can be diagnosed in many if not most cases between the second and third birthdays, and we count this group in with all other school-age children, it would add about another 800 children. If it is decided that, by analogy with deaf children, education should begin for this group from the third year of life, then this is a considerable 'extra' when taking the amount of provision needed for them (the Lindens School for instance will take children from the age of 3).

These survey figures came as a considerable surprise to most health and education authorities. It is often stated that autism is an 'extremely rare' condition. When the incidence is shown to be a little less than one in 2,000 live births, then the size of the problem is seen as more serious than previously thought.

Middlesex has a 'typical' distribution of social classes; a research quoted by Lorna Wing suggests the figures are similar for Denmark, and there is no reason to believe that this discovered incidence is at all unusual, at least in Europe.

Evaluation of autistic children's abilities by psychological testing

There are a number of studies in which intelligence quotients, reading and number abilities of autistic children have been reported. The following quotation from a paper by Lockyer and Rutter[4] is a fairly typical finding:

> the results of the present study strongly indicate that the IQ is a most useful predictor of the children's future level of intelligence and social maturity, as well as providing a measure of current performance. Furthermore, it has previously been shown that the level of IQ is an excellent predictor of the likely behavioural outcome and level of adjustment in adolescence and early adult life (p. 876).

However, they also note that 'many workers have expressed scepticism concerning the value of IQ test findings in children diagnosed psychotic'. The following are some general criticisms of research in which evaluation of the abilities of autistic children has been attempted.

1   It is exceptionally difficult to obtain and maintain rapport with an autistic child in a test situation. By definition, he does not relate to people and at best relates to but a few familiar objects. When presented with strange stimulus objects (e.g. those he is required to manipulate for test purposes) or verbal questions, he more often than not does not respond, or responds only spasmodically and with apparent indifference. One psychologist for instance, testing an autistic child of 5 on the Merrill-Palmer Scale, wrote that it took the child thirty minutes to complete putting six pegs in six holes. He concluded, partly because of this, that the child was not autistic, but severely subnormal. One wonders how involved this child was in the task, how sustained his attention, for him to take such a length of time to complete it.

2 In many of the studies the tests initially used with a child are not the same as those used at follow-up. One reason for this is that intelligence tests are designed for children in specific age groups. For instance, the Merrill-Palmer Scale is useful for testing autistic children because a total score can be obtained without using verbal items, but the age range it covers does not exceed that of young primary school children. Follow-up studies often have to assess intelligence by using a different test, such as the performance scale of the Wechsler Intelligence Test for Children. A child can, therefore, achieve a different score on two tests after a lapse of time because of the different types of items on which he has to succeed. There is also a possibility he would achieve a different IQ if he were of an age (say 5) when the two tests overlapped in age (the WISC goes from 5 to 16) and was given the two tests in the same week. Thus a drop or increase in IQ at follow-up can be caused by the use of different tests and not necessarily represent improvement or deterioration over time in general cognitive functioning.

3 A related point is that a test result (e.g. an intelligence quotient) will usually include scores of all items a child attempts. As the autistic child becomes verbally capable, he will therefore be attempting verbal items of a test where these were omitted at the earlier date because of his lack of verbal comprehension. Although verbal ability is developing in such a child, it may well be at a stage much lower than that of an average normal child at the time he is tested. If some of his performance scores have been good at the earlier testing (and some autistic children are exceptionally good at manipulation items such as jigsaws, etc.) the inclusion of scores of less well-achieved verbal items will depress the total score, when in fact the child is progressing satisfactorily in verbal abilities. The 'global' IQ score will mask such changes in the child's specific abilities.

4 Lockyer and Rutter refer to the skill demanded of the tester when administering intelligence tests to autistic children. No researches, however, mention how experienced the testers were when beginning testing such children. It is known that experienced testers can obtain significantly different scores from the same child on the same test even when

the child exhibits no disturbed behaviour. Combining this point with that made in (1), it can be seen that the chance of getting unreliable scores from autistic children (i.e. if the same child were given the same test by the same tester on two occasions in the same week) is quite high; none of the studies however mentions checks of tester reliability. Most of the follow-up studies indicate that autistic children in general do not show significant gains in IQ over a number of years. In fact they usually reveal that the IQ has remained roughly the same, or has dropped. Only one study known to the writer[5] reports substantial gains, of twenty-four IQ points eight years after initial testing. However this study is open to the criticism that different tests were used initially and at follow-up.

5   Rarely is there mention in detail of what happened to the children between testings. The Lockyer and Rutter paper states that half of the sample of sixty-three children retested were being cared for in long-stay institutions where the general quality of care they received varied considerably, 'and sometimes it was good'. Even where 'care' is 'good' this does not necessarily mean that the child is receiving appropriate specialised education and treatment. In fact, in the past, this likelihood has been remote.

6   The last point is related to the above. Until now there have been few programmes for autistic children which have demonstrated substantial educational and behavioural progress as a result of teaching-treatment. The National Society schools and the Lindens School began in the mid-1960s or later, and most of the children tested in the published reports did not have the benefit of such or similar programmes (the one exception is a study by Rutter and Bartak[6] where a three-year follow-up study included two of the schools mentioned above). The fact that children have remained in long-stay institutions to the time of follow-up investigations itself indicates that substantial progress could not have been achieved. An increasing number of autistic children are now being transferred to normal schools at younger ages, and these are the populations which will produce interesting follow-up studies. For these children, unlike those in the samples previously reported, will have had experiences in normal communities where expectations are much higher and less self-fulfilling. The

labelling involved when a child is 'given' an intelligence quotient can indeed influence what happens to him subsequently. Perhaps future studies should abandon using intelligence tests altogether; measuring a child's performance against his previous performance in specific tasks (criterion-referenced testing) is far more relevant for a child so disadvantaged in the test situation. True progress or the lack of it can then be realistically demonstrated.

Introduction to the chapters

Chapter 2 provides a description of the autistic condition, and discusses the problems entailed in doing so. The argument about whether it is useful to speak and write of autism as a single condition is still strongly debated, and the debate is likely to continue. What is of relevance here to the teacher is that she should become acquainted with the diagnostic criteria. Having done so she may then, in her daily observation of children diagnosed autistic, be able to identify features which may signify underlying problems of which the autistic features are only additional signs. Barbara Furneaux in chapter 3 underlines the importance of this for children who may need quite different treatment and teaching approaches to the ones described in this book.

Chapter 4 examines the resources necessary for effectively dealing with the autistic child in the classroom and at home. Such factors as the teacher's type of approach, the surroundings in which she works, her relationship with the children's families, and the parents' ability not just to cope with their child but to back up the teacher's work in a home programme, all interrelate in important ways. The ways in which these factors interact need constant re-evaluation according to the developing needs of the individual child.

In the central chapters of the book, Barbara Furneaux and Sybil Elgar produce a distillation of their long experience of working with autistic children. These expositions describe teaching techniques which have produced improvement in the child's behaviour and skills sometimes well beyond what was previously conceived possible.

In chapter 7 Jill Boucher and Les Scarth consider findings

from the ever-increasing amount of research on autistic children which may have implications in the classroom, since they indicate the particular problem with which the teacher working with these children may be faced. We do not consider that what may be effective in 'laboratory' conditions for small groups of children or the individual child may easily translate to the daily activity of the classroom. Nevertheless, it is considered important for the teacher not only to be acquainted with this activity, but where it appears relevant to her needs to be able to examine what will work for her, and to attempt to understand if it does not work, why this is the case. In this way she can become an important contributor to our understanding of many factors in autism which are still puzzling.

Chapter 8 deals with the services which may combine to make a total programme for the individual child. Jeanne Hertzog describes the roles of the general practitioner, paediatrician, child psychiatrist and others who can provide important contributions in the remediation of the child's condition.

The summary reviews what we know about dealing with autistic children and evaluates needs in the future for dealing with them. It will suggest that there is no one technique, professional discipline, theory of behaviour, or type of person that can best totally deal with the many problems autistic children present.

This leads to the last point of the introduction. The present book is written principally in the belief that if an autistic child is to be given the fullest and most effective help, many types of specialist may be needed in the process. Nevertheless, in our present state of knowledge it may justly be argued that the teacher's role appears to be a central one. For in a structured treatment unit she is in a very different situation from that of other professionals, who often only see the child and the parents for very limited amounts of time. The teacher who is trained to observe behaviour precisely can aid the diagnostic process itself, for she will provide a perspective in which to evaluate the child's condition and needs. She will see, for instance, the hourly and daily fluctuations in his differential reactions to adults and other children. She can create situations in which learning abilities can be assessed. Over a period of time she will be alert to judging which children will benefit from which kind of programme, and which will probably not respond to the one she is part of. For instance, she may be the first person to discover the likelihood that a child previously thought to be deaf can hear, or the reverse.

She will also be the reporter of progress to the child's parents, and a recipient of daily progress information from the home, from which she can refine and change her own dealings with the child. She can note the relative effects of other treatments such as drug dosage within the controlled situation of the classroom. There will also be an essential role for her in helping to create a home treatment programme.

By now the teacher reading this introduction who has not previously dealt with, or perhaps not even seen, autistic children may feel that working with them would be the last thing that she would like to take on. Certainly any teacher contemplating this work should visit a unit or school where autistic children are taught before embarking on it. Once she has observed autistic behaviour and taken into account the uncertainty of progress, the nature of the work compared with that in other teaching situations will at first appear onerous and even unrewarding.

In the balance there is, however, at least in the minds of the writers of this book, one overall and perhaps supreme reward. This is witnessing the most severe behaviour and learning difficulties change from such an unpromising initial state. At the start of teaching-treatment many of these children appear to be psychologically almost non-existent while physically they are indistinguishable from ordinary children. For the child to remain autistic is virtually for him to remain psychologically dead while physically his life exists as an irony. To help in the shaping process whereby the child finally begins to create his own self can bring rewards unknown to any other part of the teaching profession; the venture contains a magic of its own.

References

1   B. Bettelheim, *The Empty Fortress: Infantile Autism and the Birth of the Self*, Free Press, New York, 1967.
2   J. K. Wing (ed.), *Early Childhood Autism: Clinical, Educational and Social Aspects*, Pergamon, Oxford, 1966 edn.

3   J. K. Wing, N. O'Connor and V. Lotter, 'Autistic conditions in early
    childhood', *Br. Med. Journal*, 3, 1967, pp. 389–92.
4   L. Lockyer and M. Rutter, 'A five to fifteen year follow-up study of
    infantile psychoses', *Br. J. Psychiat.*, 115, 1959, pp. 867–82.
5   P. Mittler, S. Gillies and E. Jukes, 'Prognosis of psychotic children:
    report of a follow-up study', *Journal of Mental Deficiency Research*,
    10, 1966, pp. 73–83.
6   L. Bartak and M. Rutter, 'Special educational treatment of autistic
    children: a comparative study. I Design of study and characteristics of
    units', *J. Child Psych. and Psychiat.*, 14, 3, 1973.
    M. Rutter and L. Bartak, 'Special educational treatment of autistic
    children: a comparative study. II Follow-up findings and implications
    for services', *J. Child Psych. and Psychiat.*, 14, 4, 1973.

2 Description of the condition of autism, and theories of causation

BRIAN ROBERTS

The American psychiatrist, Leo Kanner, first described a condition in children he called autism in 1943[1] after examining eleven children whom he considered to form a group quite distinctive from other groups in the combination of symptoms they revealed.

The principal feature of these children for Kanner is their 'inability to relate to people from the beginning of life'; their 'aloofness' and 'aloneness' is seen as the most distinctive abnormality. He differentiated them from children who are categorised as 'severely subnormal' or 'severely mentally retarded' in their showing good or average abilities in certain areas, for instance musical ability. Other symptoms described are an obsessive desire for the maintenance of sameness, and a failure to use language for the purpose of communication.[2]

There has been much dispute since 1943 as to whether there is any point in labelling a child autistic. A major aspect of the problem argued about by diagnosticians is that the behaviours Kanner listed are all to be seen in other groups of children. There are seven major groups:

   (i)   deaf and partially hearing children;
  (ii) blind and partially sighted children;
 (iii) severely subnormal children;
 (iv) children with known brain damage;
  (v) children classified as childhood psychotics;
 (vi) children classified as childhood schizophrenics;
(vii) children with known dementing conditions, either arrested or progressive, due to a variety of pathological causes.

A second complicating factor is that most of these categories also overlap each other; for instance a child who is blind and deaf may be said to be severely subnormal with features of psychosis of organic origin (i.e. resulting from neurological damage).

To a large extent the problem of using the terms 'autism' and 'autistic' is a general one applying to all labels and systems of classification, especially those concerning illnesses. When a physician has isolated a group of symptoms as distinct from another group it is often possible to identify a cause or causes of the symptoms and provide cures or alleviating treatment. Looking back at the seven groups above however, it will be noticed that there are different *kinds* of label listed. Blindness and deafness refer to sensory defects. Brain damage is a condition which may result in sensory defect or a quite different dysfunction. 'Severe subnormality' is a term used to describe a person's level of ability, usually in terms of an intelligence quotient. 'Childhood psychosis' and 'childhood schizophrenia' are terms similar to 'autism' in that they describe *behaviour* said to be abnormal and with as yet unknown cause.

The name 'autism' is reserved for children with no known other condition, but who display the Kanner features, especially the first. (See appendix, end of chapter.) They may also have some other characteristics (see below). However, a blind or deaf child may be said to have 'autistic features', that is, he displays behaviour found in children said to be autistic who have no known other condition except for the display of behaviour described by Kanner and others. Similarly, some brain-damaged children and children classed as severely subnormal may display some characteristics of autism. Sometimes these behaviours are persistent, sometimes they are transient: they may only be in evidence every so often, or appear and never be seen again. This of course makes for further difficulties in diagnosis.

Yet another complicating factor lies in Kanner's phrase 'from the beginning of life'. Children do not have language from the beginning of life. Furthermore, their early behaviour is not complex enough to display the other Kanner symptoms. Here Kanner is referring to the fact that language does not appear at the time it should do, or if it does appear it is not used for communication; that the child grows extremely anxious when it is mature enough to notice changes in the environment, and so on. The outstanding features are that the child from birth never shows typically normal desire or ability to relate whether by verbal or non-verbal means. This is usually very hard to estimate of course. What one mother will interpret as a welcoming smile on the face of her baby, another will say is a product of wind! Mothers often find it extremely difficult, when trying to remember the development of their children from birth, to say whether the baby 'communicated' normally or not. In the many thousands of case histories taken of children diagnosed as autistic, there appear to be two groups: those who show no normal behaviour, except in having an unusually good or average ability in perhaps one area (but not speech), and those who *appear to have* up to two years of normal development, and then develop autistic behaviour. There is, however, still much debate about whether a child with autistic features at 2 ever showed normal communication responses, and in other abilities the norms are so wide that it is often difficult, if not impossible, to say that a child is abnormal in a particular aspect of development in his first year of life, and sometimes even in the second year. It is known, also, that mothers may be quite unreliable in giving accurate dates of the first evidence of a particular ability, especially if (1) they have a number of children, and (2) in circumstances where they are acutely worried about what is wrong with their child.

The terms 'childhood schizophrenia' and 'childhood psychosis' existed before the term 'autism'. Some children who would now be called autistic were given these labels before Kanner wrote his paper. In fact one purpose of the paper was to make a distinction between the eleven children Kanner examined and children belonging to these other groups. Since the Kanner paper the three terms have sometimes been used interchangeably, and it is necessary to discuss this issue further.

Both 'psychotic' and 'schizophrenic' are terms which describe adult mental illness. Children with the same or similar features were therefore said to have a childhood version of the same 'illness'. Unfortunately the medical profession has not always been consistent in distinguishing between 'psychosis' and the so-called 'schizophrenias'. In the childhood versions, however, many diagnosticians reserve these terms, particularly 'childhood schizophrenia', to describe children who have had at least some years of apparently normal development. 'Childhood psychosis' is often used as a blanket term to cover both children who would be diagnosed as autistic by some, and those whose normality of general development may be in doubt, and who begin to develop abnormal signs at later than 2 years.

It can be imagined that with these kinds of confusion there has indeed been much dispute since the 1940s about labelling children with severe disturbance; because of this a committee was convened in England in 1960 to examine the evidence as to how useful the distinctions noted above might be. The committee was under the chairmanship of Dr Mildred Creak, who had had a great deal of experience of such children. They listed nine points, describing the condition of 'childhood schizophrenia'. This term, some writers feel (e.g. Werry[3]), was unfortunate. Werry suggests the nine points are comprehensive enough to cover all forms of 'childhood psychosis' and notes they have become increasingly accepted as a basis for such a diagnosis, especially in that they have been incorporated almost unchanged in the classification of childhood disorders by the American Group for the Advancement of Psychiatry (GAP).

Many diagnosticians use the nine points when attempting to diagnose cases of autism; there is far more detail of description than in the Kanner list, and this factor is found helpful. An English psychiatrist, Dr Michael Rutter, notes amongst other criticisms that the committee does not specify how many of the criteria are necessary to make a diagnosis. Rutter also considers the *time* at which a feature becomes prominent is an important diagnostic factor. Most diagnosticians and writers agree that the first of the Creak points, aloneness and apparent lack of any social skills, is essential to a diagnosis of autism but some are in disagreement as to which of the other points are crucial.

Some writers (e.g. Lotter, see chapter 1, note 3) suggest that the most important are the first and fourth, while others feel that the first and ninth are essential: the viewpoint in the latter group is that this enables a distinction which excludes severely subnormal children, i.e. children who are uniformly severely retarded.

The National Society for Autistic Children (who have also published a list by Dr L. Wing of symptoms claiming to relate specifically to autistic children), lists the nine points as follows· (this is an adaptation from the original report[4] expressed in simpler language, and giving examples of the behaviour of children known to the Society as autistic):

Items of behaviour that may occur in the autistic conditions of childhood

1 *Gross and sustained impairment of emotional relation-ships with people.*
   This may show itself in one or more of the following ways:
   (a) Aloof and distant manner. The child behaves as if other human beings were just objects, and did not exist at all, unless approached in special ways by people he likes (see below).
   (b) Persistent tendency to turn away from people, or look past them *especially when spoken to* (although the child may respond with pleasure if tickled, carried, swung round, etc.).
   (c) Great difficulty in playing with other children. Sometimes complete indifference to other children.
   (d) If the condition is present from early infancy, the baby may not be 'cuddly'—that is, he may not respond to being picked up, and will not make himself ready to be picked up by stretching out his arms (although he may come to enjoy cuddling later on).
   Many parents have found that they can 'get through' to their autistic child, and have found warmth and love under the surface. However, the lack of outward signs of warmth towards people who do not know him still remains.

2 *Self-examination.*
   The child may examine parts of his body, e.g. his hands and feet, long after the baby stage. He may appear to regard them as perpetually new and

strange—for example, one child always looked at her hand, as it appeared out of her jumper sleeve when dressing, as if she had no idea it was going to emerge.

3 *Pre-occupation with particular objects, or certain characteristics of them, without regard to their accepted functions, persisting long after the baby stage.*
This can be shown in one or more of the following ways:
   (a) Making collections of all kinds of objects to carry around. Great anger and distress if any are lost.
   (b) Great attachment to one special object, such as a box, a piece of cloth, etc. Anger and distress if lost.
   (c) Making lines and patterns with all kinds of objects, regardless of their real use.
   (d) Tendency to examine objects in peculiar ways. The child may turn things over and over, bite them, scratch them or tap on them, put them close to his eyes and then far away, or twist them close to his ear as if listening. He may always spin the wheels of mechanical toys, or look through a piece of paper without looking at the picture on it.
   (e) Odd play with objects e.g. spinning them, flicking pieces of string, rattling stones in a tin, tearing paper, etc.

4 *Sustained resistance to change in the environment, and a striving to maintain order or sameness.*
This may show itself in one or more of the following ways:
   (a) Great difficulty in changing routines—disturbed behaviour if the smallest thing is changed (even if habits were difficult to form in the first place).
      Examples of the remarkably rigid routines these children may show include refusal to deviate from a usual route for the daily walk, insistence on walking straight along any road and refusing to turn any corners, refusal to wear any but familiar clothes, insistence on one type of food only. Particular difficulty may be caused by a child's refusal to

change from baby foods to solids. It may also be completely impossible to make such a child swallow medicine, since it is unfamiliar.

(b) Resistance to learning new things (although child may learn and perform well after initial resistance).

(c) Great distress if there is any change in the arrangement of familiar objects such as furniture.

5 *Behaviour leading to suspicion of abnormalities of the special senses in the absence of any obvious physical cause.*

This may show itself in one or more of the following ways:

(a)   (i) at times no reaction at all to speech or noises.

    (ii) positive attempts to get away from some noises, e.g. the child covers his ears when spoken to. Sometimes positive distress shown at some noises.

    (iii) people ask if the child is deaf even though he can hear some things very well.

(b)   (i) at times no reaction at all to things seen.

    (ii) some interest in moving things but little or no interest in stationary objects.

    (iii) positive attempts to get away from some things to be seen e.g. the child turns away or covers eyes if asked to look at something.

    (iv) People ask if child is short-sighted, or even blind, even though he can see some things very well.

(c) Apparent indifference to pain or heat or cold. The child may be quite stoical if he falls or bumps himself. He may go out with few or no clothes on in very cold weather without appearing to feel cold. He may also pick at scabs and scars or even injure himself without seeming to feel the pain.

(d) Willingness to taste or eat unusual objects may persist for years, sometimes combined with extreme food faddiness mentioned in 4(a). A child may eat coal, earth, flowers, dirty snow, plastic toys, paint, matches, etc. long after the usual age for this habit.

6 *Abnormalities of moods.*

This may show itself in one or more of the following ways:

(a) Outbursts of violent and prolonged rage and distress, shown by screams, tears, stamping, kicking, biting, etc. These outbursts may occur:

   (i) because of change of routine, loss of a wanted object, desire for forbidden food, sweets, objects for collection, etc., temporary absence of a loved person or other frustration.

   (ii) because of a special fear which may be very hard to understand — perhaps of bathing, wearing shoes, sitting on a disliked chair, etc. (although he may have no fear of real danger — see below).

   (iii) because of necessary interference from others e.g. during hair brushing and combing, washing, dressing, nail cutting, etc.

   (iv) for no discernible reason at all.

During these outbursts, which are out of all proportion to the cause, the child cannot be comforted even by somebody he knows and loves, and pushes away if cuddled — sometimes he attacks people he normally loves. These episodes often stop as suddenly as they started, if something does manage to distract the child's attention, and the mood may change in a second to cheerful calm.

(b) Periods of laughing and giggling, for which the reasons may be obscure.

(c) Lack of fear of real dangers — e.g. the child may climb on the roof, run straight into a moving swing, run into the sea fully clothed, play with fire, etc.

7 *Speech disturbances.*

This may show itself in one or more of the following ways:

(a) No speech at all. Speech may never have been present, or it may have begun and then been lost.

(b) Fragments of speech and contractions of words.

Examples are 'na' for 'Ribena', 'n'n' for 'I want', 'jiu' for 'orange juice'. These fragments may be the only speech.

(c) Very simple speech only—as for a 2-year-old.

(d) Use of 'you', 'he' or the child's name instead of 'I'.

(e) Parrot-like repetition of words, phrases, sentences or even whole poems and songs without regard to meaning.

(f) Frequent use of a 'special voice' different from that of the normal one, sometimes with special peculiarities of pronunciation.

(g) Strange pedantic type of speech.

In general, the child has difficulty in communicating all but the simplest needs by means of speech. He may prefer to take another person by the hand and show them what he wants instead of asking.

8 *Disturbances of movements and general activity.*
This may show itself in one or more of the following ways:

(a) Great over-activity—running up and down, without ever tiring. This may be marked at night. The child may stay awake very late, sometimes playing happily, sometimes crying or screaming. He may not settle to sleep till midnight or later. Other children may wake during the night and cry, refusing any comfort. Yet others wake and play for hours in the night, apparently without any desire for company. Despite the lack of sleep, they usually seem full of energy in the day.

(b) Immobility—the child may lie completely still with no movement at all for long periods.

(c) Special movements:
   (i) rocking
   (ii) head banging
   (iii) jumping
   (iv) twisting, flapping and writhing of arms and legs—especially when excited
   (v) spinning
   (vi) facial grimaces of all kinds

      (vii) odd ways of walking e.g. on tip-toe
   (viii) unusual hand movements e.g. turning hand
         with outstretched fingers in front of face
    (ix) constant repetitions of the same movement
     (x) extreme pleasure in bodily movement such as
         swinging, rocking, riding in cars, etc.

9 *A background of serious retardation in which islets of
normal, near normal, or exceptional intellectual
function or skill may appear.*
This means that, on the whole, the child is well behind
his age group in the things he can do. Where other
children of his age may be fairly independent, able to
go out alone, do shopping, visit the cinema, etc., the
autistic child usually needs his mother's attention and
supervision all or most of the time, because he cannot
look after himself and keep himself out of danger.

On the other hand, he may be able to do one or a
few things remarkably well, such as:
(a) calculations
(b) jigsaws and puzzles
(c) singing and remembering music, and pleasure in
listening to all kinds of music
(d) reading and writing
(e) memorising long lists of dates, names, poems, odd
facts, etc.
(f) special mechanical skills.
(Many other examples could be given.)

In addition to the positive abnormalities listed above,
the diagnosis of autism depends just as much upon
noting what the children do *not* do. The most
important gaps in their development are as follows:

1 The children do not show any eagerness to
communicate with other people, apart from asking
for needs, or in some cases, talking on repetitive
themes. Even if they have a wide vocabulary, they do
not enjoy conversing with others just for the pleasure
of chatting.

2 They do not show the non-autistic child's lively
curiosity about people and things. A few autistic

children collect facts about certain subjects, but this
is quite unlike the desire to find out about all kinds of
things that characterise normal human behaviour, and
which can be seen in non-autistic retarded people also.
3 Autistic children have no imaginative 'pretend' play,
or, rather rarely, they concentrate on one single
theme only in their play and are not influenced by
suggestions from other people.

The National Society's pamphlet also notes that:

all normal children can show any of the behaviour
described at some stage in their lives. They can at times
be withdrawn, obsessional, have temper trantrums, cling
to special objects, etc. — these are just aspects of any
child's development. The autistic child, however, shows
the behaviour in the list above for years on end,
and — most important of all — *he does virtually nothing
else at all* (until he begins to emerge from his illness). His
oddness stands out all day and every day, not just now
and again, or when he is not feeling well.

This point has been emphasised because it is extremely
important that a child going through a difficult phase,
but who will eventually develop normally should not be
given a label which has such far reaching implications.

This last point is an 'extremely important' one indeed, but in
itself contains another problem. For autistic children (i.e.
children who are extremely remote in their behaviour, etc.)
may not show the Creak symptoms with equal intensity or frequency. Further, some will display some of the symptoms and
not others; rarely are all nine seen in all children said to be
autistic. It can be seen therefore that under the 'umbrella'
term 'autism' there will be children displaying *different combinations of symptoms.* What appears to be crucial to most
diagnosticians, however, is the presence of symptoms corres-
ponding to Creak points 1 and 9, and possibly 4, and some of
the other symptoms, all in severe form and of enduring
nature. Nevertheless, it is necessary to point out that the
writers in this book have all seen children who might be classi-

31

fied as 'borderline autistic' children where behaviour satisfies the criteria although symptoms are not severe. These are usually children who, with no other known dysfunction, are beginning to relate in relatively normal manner to others and to their environments generally, but simultaneously show some bizarre behaviour. It may be the case that prior to being seen their condition was more severe, but this is often difficult to estimate in view of the previously noted difficulties of obtaining accurate information on the child's development. In the present state of experience and knowledge of the conditions of autism it does seem to be the case that the autistic child in his severest state is, as Kanner claimed, quite distinct from other disturbed children. It will be clear to the reader by now that great care has to be taken by the diagnostician, in deciding that the child is not one whose behaviour is a reaction to stress as a result of a primary dysfunction such as deafness, which is sometimes quite difficult to detect, especially in view of Creak point 5(a)(i) above.

The last question, therefore, is at what age can a judgment be made that a child's condition is severe enough to be 'quite distinct' from that of other conditions? It has been pointed out that early in life he will not have enough differentiated behaviour to qualify for any of the Creak points. It is only as behaviour matures and abilities and dispositions *should be* in evidence, that we can notice a delay or anomaly. Unfortunately there are wide differences between child and child in terms of the appearance of abilities at a very young age. There may be, for instance, a difference of a year in the onset of speech in two children of the same family, both of whom turn out to be of normal development and record similar IQs at a later date. A child may show lags in certain aspects of his development, as in the old wives' tale 'early walker, slow talker'. In the latter case the 'lag' may be followed by a 'spurt' in speech. A mother of a child with little or no speech may take her child to her GP only to be told of such discrepancies at, say, twenty-four months, and a 'wait and see' policy is proposed. For the majority of children this will be harmless and speech will ensue rapidly in the third year. However, if the doctor is cautious, he will perhaps look at other areas (e.g. hearing, vision), consider the Kanner and Creak points, etc., note any other signs of delayed development and refer on to other specialists if he has cause for suspicion of abnormality; but such is the confusion in the descriptions and definitions of autism that the other specialists, for instance, child psychiatrists, paediatricians and psychologists, may be similarly unwilling to give an early diagnosis of autism. They themselves may adopt a wait and see policy. Such a situation may continue until the time arrives for the child to begin schooling, and valuable time may be lost in helping the child and his family to overcome the overwhelming problems they face.

With this in mind, psychologists have been attempting to develop diagnostic procedures which are sensitive to distinguishing between the psychoses of childhood and which are reliable in relating significant symptoms in very early infancy to conditions which are more easily recognised at a later age. Bernard Rimland has such a check-list in the appendix to his book *Infantile Autism* (Appleton-Century-Crofts, 1964). Since this publication the check-list has been continuously revised in view of the large amount of data he is receiving from parents of autistic children and those with similar conditions. Ongoing research by four Australian psychologists using the Rimland list has recently shown[5] that abnormal responses to sensory stimuli, for instance under-reaction or over-reaction to lights, colours or sounds, are important diagnostic features of what they call 'early onset psychosis'. Another feature, which Kanner also noted (see appendix on pages 39–41), is the failure of the child to reach out or to prepare himself before being picked up, i.e. lack of anticipatory behaviour. The writers point out that awareness of the possible importance of these observable symptoms on the part of those who see the child in early infancy, notably the parents, health visitors, and family physicians, could lead to earlier diagnosis and the beginning of treatment. If such and similar research projects continue to establish such findings, then there is no doubt that we should soon have much more accurate means of detecting the possibility that a child has a major disorder. In addition the rightness or otherwise of using such terms as 'autism', 'childhood schizophrenia', etc. will be validated or invalidated. The realistic use of these labels depends upon adequate demonstration that groups of symptoms do exist together in

33

some children in a way that is different from the way symptoms are grouped in other cases or conditions.

Aetiology of autism

This section gives a brief outline of some theories and researches which indicate a cause or causes of the condition of autism; up to the present none of them has provided sufficiently strong evidence for specific causes.

The original 1943 paper by Kanner, and subsequent ones by him and other researchers (e.g. Eisenberg and Kanner[6]) have appeared to implicate parents, especially the mother, as a strong if not total causative factor in the onset and maintenance of autism in their child. Kanner in his first paper found the parents of his eleven children to be intelligent, sophisticated, emotionally cold, distant, impersonal and obsessional. Eisenberg in another study claimed to find 85 per cent of the fathers of autistic children to have serious personality difficulties which he thought might affect the nature of their relationships with their children. In a different context, however, Eisenberg[7] disclaims any bias in this direction on Kanner's behalf, and points out that in the 1943 article Kanner wrote that 'here we seem to have a pure culture example of *inborn* autistic disturbances of affective contact' (Eisenberg's italics). Nevertheless, as Eisenberg points out in the same lecture, there was a 'psychogenic bias' as he calls it, in the USA in the 1940s and 1950s. The child's mother was said to be largely if not totally responsible for his condition. She was labelled by some writers the 'schizophrenogenic mother' or 'refrigerator mother' who did not know how, or did not bother, to relate to her child. It was usually not stated at what stage of the child's development the mother was supposed to have affected the child's behaviour: it was presumed she 'caused' the condition in an ongoing way from birth.

This explanation has severe limitations. There are reports of children subjected to severe hostility, rejection and indifference on the part of their parents or parent surrogates which cause disturbance in their offspring which is not of an autistic nature. There are studies of children brought up from birth in institutions with minimal amounts of contact with either adults or other children where none of the children is said to show autistic behaviour (but equally there are reports of children in institutions who became autistic). In such environments the resulting disorder is often noted as apathy and 'anaclitic depression' (a slowing of development, weeping, sadness, and an increased susceptibility to disease).

Other writers suggest that the causative factor is not a single one; a particular combination of factors is said to have caused the condition. Some theorists for instance suggest that the child is born with a vulnerability—predisposing factors present at birth—which, in combination with environmental factors, causes autism. One suggestion is that children later diagnosed autistic are born with particularly well-developed hearing and vision. As they learn about the world in the first place through the senses, they are thought to be especially vulnerable to something going wrong in the environment if these modalities are more attuned and sensitive than in the average child. The dull child would not notice such factors at all, so this type of explanation suggests. An obvious problem with this explanation is that it does not account easily for autistic behaviour in children known to be severely retarded from birth and those who show defects in sensory channels.

It may be argued, however, that this group is responding to *internal* malfunctions: the sensory equipment the child is born with and through which he comes to apprehend the world does not cope adequately with the information he receives. Lauretta Bender, for instance, thinks of psychotic behaviour as being what she calls a primitive mode of defence against a variety of internal and external pathologies.[8] Goldfarb,[9] writing about 'childhood schizophrenics' (though in some writing he refers to them as psychotic), specifically implicates the central nervous system, pointing to the possibility of deficits of perception and faulty integration of different aspects of the nervous system.

Bernard Rimland, in his book *Infantile Autism*, gives an extensive review of the literature on causation, and concludes that the primary cause may well be a lesion in the reticular activating system (RAS). This is a structure in the core of the brain stem known to influence arousal, attention and sleep. He says the lesion must occur during pregnancy or in the period around birth, and results in too little arousal in the child's nervous system for him to make sense of the world. The RAS, he asserts, is a function basic to all cognition in making sense and utilisation of incoming information.

Hutt and Hutt[10] suggest the opposite: that the defect in the RAS is one which produces great arousal in the child, and therefore causes a blocking of incoming information and sensations. The Hutts based this conclusion not only from observation of the behaviour of autistic children, but also from the patterns of brain activity which electroencephalograph recordings registered of their group of children. They found these patterns to be distinctive and different from those of normal children. However, there are a number of problems in recording brain activity, and this finding is not regarded as conclusive evidence either for abnormal brain activity or for involvement of the RAS. The research is important nevertheless, for it points to further development of this kind of enquiry. Rimland's conclusions were based apparently purely on speculation related to his observation of autistic behaviour. The problem is that sometimes a child will behave as though he is blocking out sensation (for instance, putting his fingers in his ears, not looking at anything or anyone directly), and sometimes as if he is deliberately seeking it, as in obsessional play with water, switching electric lights on and off, and so on. Some children only do one or the other; some do both at different times: neither of these explanations appears to fit the behaviour of all children who would be diagnosed under the Kanner or Creak criteria.

Deslauriers and Carlson[11] produced a theory a year or two later which appears to explain both these types of behaviour, as well as other characteristics of the autistic child. Both the RAS and the limbic system are said by them to be involved. The limbic system is a midbrain area associated with self-stimulation. For instance, when animals have electrodes implanted in the limbic area they forego food, water and sleep because, it is hypothesised, the stimulated limbic activity is so rewarding. Deslauriers and Carlson postulate a model of what they call a 'two arousal system'. Normally there should be a balance between the workings of the two systems in terms of appropriate dealing with incoming environmental stimuli and those deriving from the body. They suggest that, because the 'setting' of the two arousal systems can be faulty, either too high or too low, the child is either under- or over-sensitive to different stimuli. There may be deprivation of adequate stimulation, distortion of the reception of stimulation, or the child may be overloaded.

This certainly tallies with the description of some of the behaviour noted on page 27 in describing the Creak criteria 5(a) and 5(b). Whether it accounts for all the behaviour is disputable; the theory is complex and flexible enough to appear a promising area for development, though unlike the Hutts' work it is not yet based on research findings. Deslauriers and Carlson argue that it is suggestive in terms of treatment strategies. However, the treatment illustrated in their book was carried out before they arrived at their theory of causation, which is in fact a development of Routtenberg's ideas.

British researchers have similarly looked at aspects of autism which would appear to have implications for education and treatment. Jill Boucher and Les Scarth discuss these researches in another chapter. It remains to be noted here that the work of O'Connor, Hermelin, Frith and others appear to implicate dysfunctions in sensory modalities as the major defects. These researchers, however, do not seem to be as concerned with searching for causative explanations of autism so much as enquiring into what specific malfunction the autistic child has to cope with and how the situation may be remedied.

One final issue regarding etiology remains for discussion. This is the presence (noted at the beginning of the chapter) of autistic features shown by other groups of handicapped children, for instance blind and partially sighted, deaf and partially hearing children. The question that is often asked is whether the autistic features are a reaction to a primary condition? If we think this to be the case, then by analogy it may be argued that something like the explanation suggested by Deslauriers and Carlson would appear to be the most promising. The *behaviour* may well be a reaction to a primary condition, such as blindness or deafness; but not all, or by any means a majority of the blind, the deaf, the brain-damaged, etc. have autistic features. Perhaps there is something in the combination of initial damage and the child's early handling which is

37

the precipitating cause in those cases where there are such combinations of symptoms. For example, children who give few if any cues as to how to handle them, especially to a mother experiencing her first child, will rarely get handled 'correctly'—whatever the correct way to handle such children is. Deslauriers suggests that the autistic child is one who has never experienced affective contact because he has never had the capacity to experience it. Such a capacity, he noted, is related to those perceptual abilities through which the child comes to understand his world. Without them, he cannot make sense of it, and the people responding to him make no sense of his behaviour. If the child makes no sense of his mother's touch, warmth, nutritional supply, sounds, etc., and reacts without apparent interest no matter what the mother does in response, it is not surprising that this will evoke confusion, anxiety, and perhaps a defensive indifference ultimately in the mother. She will perhaps desperately look forward to having a normal child. Even when the mother has normal children as well as an autistic child, she will still feel very different from the mother of normal children, and different also in some ways from the mother of a child with other kinds of handicap. She will perhaps have been told many conflicting things about her child, especially in relation to the causes of the condition. One mother I know claims she was told bluntly by the general practitioner 'you've caused this'. Even if the mother has no such ideas, there will be much perplexity and sheer weariness in coping with her child, and this will be evident in her responses to others. She may suppress the evidence with a cheerful smile, but this usually masks the experience of years of bewilderment.

The teacher meeting such a mother for the first time is likely to experience her as 'abnormal'. It would be odd if this were not the case. The mother may be looking for somebody to resolve all the confusion that is the result of what she has been told by the different 'experts'.

It will be seen from what is written above that there is as yet no clear evidence which will resolve the problems autistic children pose. There are obvious dangers in discussing causative factors and treatment issues, in the kind of statement, unfortunately not uncommon, that there is a simple cause and therefore possibly a simple solution to dealing with the problem of autism. Examples are: 'he's missed out on love, and therefore needs loving' (often known as cuddle therapy), or 'his condition is probably caused by a chemical factor, so we need to look for the right drug, B6 or B12 or some such' (chemotherapy) as though the ingestion of a chemical will produce speech in the child and a rapid reversion to or imitation of normal social responses.

These simplicities can only in the long run produce despair in the ever-hoping parent. This chapter has attempted to show some of the complexity of the problem we are dealing with; it also notes some aspects of the problem that are becoming increasingly agreed on.

Appendix: 'The Kanner Criteria'

Writers referring to 'the Kanner criteria' often mention them as being three, four or five in number (e.g. Lotter *et al.* [12]). The difficulty here lies in knowing which of the Kanner papers these writers are referring to. It has recently become possible to compare his papers easily in the excellent collection, *Childhood Psychosis: Initial Studies and Insights* (Winston, 1973).

On this writer's (Brian Roberts) count, the 1943 paper (i.e. the earliest one) lists about ten diagnostic points; it is difficult to put an exact number on them. Kanner in this paper used a system of italics, not numbers, and some of the italicised headings appear related. However, it appears that Kanner regards some of these 'points' as not altogether essential, and patently some of them, e.g. 'good cognitive potentialities' and 'physically essentially normal' are only of significance when combined with other diagnostic criteria.

The factors he mentioned in the 1943 paper are as follows (in the order Kanner presents them):

1 'Inability to relate themselves in the ordinary way to people and situations from the beginning of life. . . . There is, from the start, an extreme autistic aloneness that, whenever possible, disregards, ignores, shuts out anything that comes to the child

from the outside.' This Kanner terms as the outstanding 'pathognomoic fundamental disorder'.

2 'Failure to assume at any time an anticipatory posture preparatory to being picked up.'

3 Either no speech or 'failure to use language to convey meaning to others'.

4 'Excellent rote memory', language being 'deflected in a considerable measure to a self-sufficient semantically and conversationally valueless or grossly distorted memory exercise'.

5 'Personal pronouns are repeated just as heard so he comes to speak of himself as "you" and of the person addressed as "I".'

6 'Not only the words but the intonation [of the person speaking to the child] is retained.'

7 Refusal of food. Most of the sample Kanner notes 'after an unsuccessful struggle . . . finally gave up . . . and all of a sudden began eating satisfactorily'.

8 'Another intrusion comes from loud noises and moving objects which are, therefore, reacted to with horror.'

9 'The child's noises are anxious and all of his performances are as monotonously repetitive as are his verbal utterances. . . . The child's behaviour is governed by an anxiously obsessive desire for the maintenance of sameness.'

10 The autistic child 'has a good relation to objects, he is interested in them, can play happily with them for hours.'

11 'They are all [i.e. his original sample of eleven children] unquestionably endowed with good cognitive potentialities. They all have strikingly intelligent physiognomies. Their faces . . . give the impression of serious-mindedness and, in the presence of others, an anxious tenseness.'

12 'Physically, the children were essentially normal.'

13 'They all come of highly intelligent families.'

In his joint paper with Eisenberg[13] he lists five distinctive features:

1 'Extreme detachment from human relationships' (they mention the failure to assume anticipatory posture in this paragraph).

2 'Failure to use language for the purpose of communication.'

3 'Anxiously obsessive desire for the maintenance of sameness, resulting in a marked limitation in the variety of spontaneous activity.'

4 'Fascination for objects . . . handled with skill in fine motor movements.'

5 'Good cognitive potentialities.'

Eisenberg and Kanner go on to note that, 'in the light of experience with a ten-fold increase in clinical material [by 1955 they had seen more than 120 children diagnosed as autistic] we would now isolate . . . two pathognomic features, both of which must be present, extreme self-isolation and obsessive insistence on the preservation of sameness, features that may be regarded as primary.' They go on to say, 'the vicissitudes of language development . . . may be seen as derivatives of the basic disturbance in human relatedness.'

Thus the number of essential features have more than halved in their 1956 discussion, and three of the points (2, 4 and 5) are now apparently not considered as essential features. From Eisenberg and Kanner's exposition it appears that the reason for these reductions is that some of the other symptoms overlap with other conditions, the instances they give being those of severe retardation and childhood schizophrenia.

References

1 L. Kanner, 'Autistic disturbances of affective contact', *Nervous Child* 2, 1943, pp. 217–50.

2 See the appendix on pages 39–41 for full list of Kanner's diagnostic points.

3 J. S. Werry, 'Childhood psychosis' in H. C. Quay and J. S. Werry, *Psychopathological Disorders of Childhood*, Wiley, New York, 1972.

4 K. Cameron, *et al.*, *Schizophrenic Syndrome in Childhood*, progress report (April 1961) of a Working Party.

5 M. Prior, D. Boulton, C. Gajzago and D. Perry, 'The classification of childhood psychoses by numerical toxonomy', *J. Child Psychol., Psychiat.*, 16, 1975, pp. 321–30.

6   L. Eisenberg and L. Kanner, 'Early infantile autism', *Amer. J. Orthopsychiat*, 26, 1956.

7   L. Eisenberg in M. Rutter (ed.), *Infantile Autism: Concepts, Characteristics and Treatment*, Churchill, London, 1971.

8   She usually calls the children schizophrenic, but from descriptions she gives of the children seen, they obviously include those we would now call autistic.

9   W. Goldfarb, *Childhood Schizophrenia*, Harvard University Press, 1961.

10   C. Hutt, S. J. Hutt, D. Lee and C. Ounsted, 'Arousal and childhood autism', *Nature*, 204, 1964, pp. 908 ff.

11   A. Deslauriers and C. Carlson, *Your Child is Asleep: Early Infantile Autism*, Dorsey Press, Homewood, Illinois, 1969.

12   J. K. Wing, N. O'Connor and V. Lotter, 'Autistic conditions in early childhood', *Br. Med. Journal*, 3, 1967, pp. 389–92.

13   Eisenberg and Kanner, op. cit., pp. 55–65.

3 Differential diagnosis

BARBARA FURNEAUX

Sally was admitted to a special school for seriously disturbed and psychotic children when she was 6 years old. She was a pretty, plump little girl with fair curly hair, bright blue eyes and a very sweet smile. She had a few words of speech, would happily join in, and try to sing nursery rhymes and enjoyed all musical activities. She would attempt to use simple nursery sense-training apparatus and could feed herself in a rather messy way. She was, however, totally un-toilet-trained. Although she had never previously attended school, or been parted from her mother for any period of time, she left her without any sign of distress or disturbance even on her first day. Nor did she make any open sign of recognising that her mother had left her. Even when school had become familiar she never wanted to play with the other children, neither did she seek out the company of adults; but, if one sat near her, Sally would clamber on to her lap and hold her rather as a baby monkey clings on to its mother. Any change of room or even of the furniture in a room was disliked by her and if left alone and unstimulated she would have been perfectly happy to sit in her own particular chair for hours on end making odd little finger-movements which usually culminated in a sudden clapping and bowing gesture, and what could only be described as a 'splutter' of apparent laughter. The only times she reacted quickly and spontaneously were when somebody produced some sweets anywhere in the room. Then she was off like a flash and was so determined to get the sweets she would even attempt to force open another child's mouth to take the sweet which they had started to eat.

Jeffrey was also 6 when he first went to school. He was tall for his age, awkward in all his movements and with a very odd,

43

unstable gait. He was extremely demanding of adult attention, and frequently fell into noisy tantrums if he could not
monopolise it. On the other hand he would hit himself and
become very upset if any other child in the room showed any
sign of noisy behaviour. He had a little laboured speech and,
provided he had constant individual stimulus, he could do
many of the simple pieces of infant apparatus. Unlike Sally, he
hated music, and would become very distressed whenever he
heard it. On the other hand he resembled Sally in his odd
finger-movements and hand stereotypies. He was toilet-
trained and could feed himself; but again, to achieve these
things he needed constant individual stimulus. Jeffrey never
played freely and spontaneously either with toys or with the
other children.

Terry was a year older when he was admitted to school, a
lovable 'roly-poly' boy who was intensely socialised and very
responsive to all personal overtures either from adults or children. He had no speech, was totally un-toilet-trained and, like
Sally, was a very messy eater. With great persistence and
patience on the part of his teachers and with constant individual attention, Terry could be helped to do very simple nursery apparatus; but as soon as he was left to carry on with this
on his own he would wander off, to sit, cross-legged in a
'comfy' chair, where he would rock backwards and forwards
with some head rolling, as he chuckled away to himself. However, from time to time, the picture would suddenly change.
The contented head rolling and chuckling would stop, as
Terry began to turn his head sideways squinting and squeezing
the lid of one eye. After a few seconds he would start to scream
and cry out loudly, kicking out with both legs, as he fiercely
banged away at his head. All that could be done when these
episodes started was to try to get near enough to him to hold
him securely, and in such a way as to try to prevent him from
damaging himself.

Jenny and Lucy were even older before they started at the
school, for they were both 8 years old. Lucy had gone first to
an ordinary infants' school, but was soon excluded because the
teachers felt they 'could not get through to her'. Jenny had
gone to a pre-school playgroup where it became obvious that
she would be quite unable to meet the demands of even a sym-

pathetic infants' school. Both Jenny and Lucy's parents, for different reasons, found it difficult to accept that their children were sufficiently disturbed to make ordinary school unsuitable for them, and this factor alone accounted for part of the delay in their being recommended to the special school they needed. Jenny was very tiny and apparently very sweet and complying. She proved, however, to have a will of iron when anything was requested of her that she did not wish to do. She had very little speech and extremely faulty articulation. She constantly sought to join the adults in all situations, appearing to feel that this was where she belonged and not with the older children. She presented gross and continuing feeding problems, as she insisted on trying to refuse all food, including sweets. At the same time she was openly angry with other children who were refusing food and, if left unchecked, would attempt to force them to eat. Her teeth were very decayed, perhaps not surprisingly, since she refused to let the dentist examine them, and, when he tried gently to persist, bit him as fiercely as the state of her teeth would allow. Superficially, Lucy was a far gentler child. She was a pale, pretty little girl with constant dark shadows under her eyes, although her parents reported that she slept well, and medical investigations established that she had no kidney disorder. Her only form of speech was incessant echolalia. Once she had grasped and repeated a phrase she would persist in repeating the same phrase over and over, until she had produced a state of despair and frustration in the person attempting to work with her. She could do 'copy-writing', simple mechanical arithmetic and simple jigsaws. All her drawings and clay models were simple stereotypes. She was uninterested in other children, displayed visual and auditory avoidance and either ignored adults, or attempted to monopolise them. These contrary responses were totally non-selective.

Jamey and Ned, both aged 6 on admission, were as interestingly contrasted as Jenny and Lucy proved to be. Jamey could never be still, Ned stood rigidly in a corner. Jamey kept up a constant babble of irrelevant, largely echolalic speech, although this was at times suddenly interspersed with an extremely relevant comment or interjection. An amusing example of this occurred during musical games. When the children sang 'Now you're married we wish you joy', Jamey called out 'Right, into bed, off with your nightie.' No one enquired too closely into the origins of this piece of echolalia! More interestingly and importantly he would appear at times to be very sensitive to the inner emotions of the adults with him, and would suddenly ask, for example, 'Why are you sad today?' or 'Got a headache?' and these apparently intuitive questions were normally an accurate reflection of the adult's mood. Ned, on the contrary, was totally mute, and even when very aroused emotionally would only utter sounds through his tightly closed lips. Jamey had an attention span of approximately one second and while normally apparently happy with the people he knew, he burst easily into tears with very little or no obvious cause. He showed constant and consistent gaze aversion, sweated easily and profusely and became desperately agitated whenever anyone unexpected went into his classroom. He would try to retreat behind the teacher, or behind a book or magazine which he would snatch up and wildly flap for as long as the visitor stayed in the room. Ned, when he could be enticed out of his corner, showed a great ability to be totally absorbed in anything that captured his interest, and it needed a very traumatic or dramatic incident for him to show any sign of emotion whatever. He also, literally, stank for he wore day and night all the clothes, including Wellington boots, which he had been dressed in when the family had changed house for the fifth time in a very short period a few weeks before he started school. He was also practically unwashed, since any attempt on the part of his parents to wash or to change him led to such panic on his part, and despair on theirs that they had literally 'given up'.

There are many other children I would like to describe to you if space would allow, but I will finish with just one more—Jill at 6 years old, a very petite, delicate looking little blonde. She was totally withdrawn, totally speechless, totally un-toilet-trained. Like Jenny she presented us with constant feeding problems. She incessantly displayed hand stereotypies and acute visual and auditory avoidance. Jill showed no sign of emotion in any circumstances whatever, her despairing and depressed mother claimed that she was 'nothing to Jill but a disciplined machine used to supply her needs'. In spite of her fragile appearance Jill proved to be very strong and tough. She was also incredibly agile and skilful in all her body movements. If at any time an adult did not immediately respond to her attempts physically to manipulate them to get her something she could not get for herself, she would fling herself to the ground in a screaming rigid frenzy, whirling around and around and from one side of the room to another with the most incredible speed, but never, at any time, even in these rages, knocking into or over any obstacle in her path.

From the above descriptions it can be seen that these children displayed a wide variety of problems, yet they had all been sent to the school with one diagnostic label—they had all been designated 'autistic children'. It is true that some of these children had some of their symptoms in common, it is also true that they displayed them to a severe degree. It has been argued, and with some practical validity, that an inaccurate label has served some useful purpose if it ensures that a child is thereby admitted to a special school. While the present degree of inadequacy of overall provision persists, and as long as a child's suitability for a certain type of special education is largely determined by a medical diagnosis, this argument cannot be totally dismissed. Nevertheless, the use of it not only tends to conceal true deficiencies in the services available, but can only lead to:

1 problems for the receiving school;
2 inadequate or unsuitable provision being made for the child and, all too frequently;
3 additional heartbreak for anxious parents who perhaps have to be told at a later stage that the diagnosis they have accepted for their child is incorrect and a less 'hopeful' one, in prognostic terms, substituted for it.

A physical parallel may serve to illustrate the weaknesses of labelling on the basis of an insufficient number of established, and clearly defined symptoms. Many illnesses have certain features, such as a high temperature, general malaise, and some form of rash or spots in common; but no doctor would ever say that a patient presenting with some of these symptoms must therefore be suffering from any specific one of the possible illnesses. Put very simply, it is just not the case that anyone with a fever and a rash must, for example, be suffering from scarlet fever. It is totally accepted that much finer distinctions must be made and every possible symptom taken account of before a true diagnosis can be given. Unfortunately, it is because the same high standards of diagnostic procedures are not generally observed in mental illnesses that a diagnosis such as autism is frequently applied so loosely that it has practically lost any of the validity it ever appeared to have.

The reasons why this has occurred are being discussed in another chapter of this book and so will not be gone into at length in this one. Briefly, however, they chiefly stem from two main causes. First, because there has been a growing tendency to ignore the basic premise stated initially by Kanner,[1] who first described and designated the possible syndrome of 'early infantile autism', and later by the working party set up at Great Ormond Street Hospital, under the chairmanship of Dr Mildred Creak,[2] which was, that the children referred to had to show the symptoms in the absence of any detectable organic damage. Second, because of the inevitable subjective nature of the assessment of, for example, the degree of severity of any of the observed symptoms.

For the rest of this chapter we shall be returning to the children described at the beginning of it, and looking more closely at their own individual symptoms and subsequent history.

A teacher in a special school has a very special role to play in addition to all his/her obvious and usually accepted duties. He is in a unique position to make observations of a child throughout several hours of the day when the child is both normally and naturally occupied, and reacting to and interacting with all the stimuli which occur. No doctor can in any circumstances have this particular advantage. In establishing a true diagnosis, therefore, the teacher and the doctor both have vital and complementary parts to play. The teacher can, and must, devise and apply on-going assessment procedures — he cannot, in any circumstances, diagnose. However, he can learn how and what observations should be made, and then referred to the relevant specialist for detailed investigation. Many disciplines might be involved in the detailed investigations as, for example, psychologists, audiologists, psychiatrists, paediatricians, and the school dentist (I have vivid memories of a psychotic child whose fierce face-smacking was dismissed by her GP as being 'one of the things psychotic children do', and who proved to have two highly septic teeth!) and they should all be available as a matter of course. Teachers do sometimes tend to be too unaware of either the need for, or the possibility of calling upon, these services.

The specialists on the other hand, are often accused of failing to communicate fully with either the teachers or even the parents, although they both have such close day-to-day knowledge and information to offer about the child.

Careful and regularly recorded observations of Sally, Jeffrey and the others soon caused the validity and usefulness of the diagnosis of autism to be questioned.

Over a few months Sally's physical and mental condition began to show signs of deterioration. She began to lose the small skills and achievements she had, and even to become too listless and lethargic to react when the sweets appeared. More and more as she tried to sit at a table she would flop forward on to the table almost as if her head was becoming too heavy to hold up. She showed signs of drooping to one side and as time went on there was a measurable difference between the circumference of her leg and arm on one side and the other. She became an ever more 'messy' eater, as if her hand could no longer find her mouth, and eventually she had to be fed. The doctors were alerted as soon as these symptoms were noticed by the teachers and a detailed physical investigation was initiated. Sally's story does not have a happy ending. She proved to have an incurable deteriorating illness which ultimately necessitated hospitalisation and intensive care as the illness took its course. Even when Sally first was admitted to the school some of the symptoms which later developed so sadly were already present. It seems fair to ask why, in the circumstances, no real physical investigations were initiated before the diagnosis of autism was given to the parents and to the school. One possible, partial, explanation may well be that there is a tendency for any specialist to interpret the less seriously displayed symptoms in the terms of his own speciality.

Jeffrey, Terry and Jamey also ultimately proved to be suffering from irreparable organic damage, of different kinds and degrees of severity. Jeffrey proved to be a case of infantile gigantism, Terry to have massive brain-damage. Jamey proved to have some degree of brain-damage and also some amount of biochemical disorder. Ned, Jenny and Lucy all proved to be seriously emotionally disturbed, but their disturbances were not psychotic. Of all the children described one only, Jill, proved to conform to the classic picture of the autistic child.

Since all these children originally given the same diagnostic label proved to have such a range of disorders, it is obvious that they all required different forms of approaches and teaching. Many teachers and others working with very disturbed or handicapped children and presented with problems totally new to their experience, not unnaturally try to look for a 'blue-print' or guide-lines as to how to tackle the apparent problem. Such 'blue-prints' do exist for different forms of handicaps; but what if, as in the cases described, the original diagnosis does not prove to be the correct one? The consequences of trying to help a child in a way described to be suitable for a child suffering from another disorder altogether are obvious.

The suggestion being made is that the first task to be tackled by anyone involved in helping handicapped children is to attempt to establish the prime nature of their handicap and to evolve the correct way to help each child accordingly. In my experience it is never sufficient to assume that the diagnosis the child is sent to you with is necessarily the correct and conclusive one. Diagnosis must be an on-going procedure. Initially therefore, the teacher is not only observing and noting anything which must be referred for specialist investigation and in so doing never overlooking the need to have eliminated all physical possibilities before deciding upon a psychological explanation, but she or he must also be getting to know and understand the child as an individual with his own abilities, idiosyncracies and temperament. All of these things are a necessary part of true diagnosis. For some of them the teacher is, as already stated, dependent upon specialist advice to which he has contributed by his careful observations, for others he should be able to rely upon his own professional expertise and experience. Practically, he has the child present and hence the immediate need to do something!

Many people feel that one of the first questions to be

answered with the kind of children being considered in this book is whether the child is indeed autistic, using the word in its classical meaning — or subnormal with, possibly, psychotic overtones. In this area the teacher can find possible cues — by, for example, making the following kinds of observations:

Does this child respond — or not respond?

If he does respond:

1   How complete is his response?
2   Does he respond consistently and in the same manner?
3   Is his response appropriate or bizarre in character?
4   What is the normal speed of his responses?
5   Has he the ability to follow through his response and in an appropriate manner?
6   Can he, when responding, go from one thing to another?
7   How well, and for how long, does he retain information?
8   Can he apply this information in a new set of circumstances?

In interpreting your observations on these points it is useful to remember that a subnormal child tends to be slow, and very limited but fairly consistent in his attempts to respond in an appropriate manner. He usually lacks the ability to develop his responses or to generalise from them. An autistic child, on the other hand, if he does respond is very likely to give a bizarre response. A very simple experiment will demonstrate this. If you put the child into the centre of a squared climbing frame and then call him to come to you, a subnormal child on the whole will be willing to do this, but unable to solve the problem of how to do it. You will need to go to him and teach him over and over again exactly how to climb through the bars and out in the simplest possible way. An autistic child, on the other hand (if he decides to comply at all), will invent the most intricate and constantly varying ways to get through and out of the frame. The exception to this would be the child who was both autistic and severely subnormal — fortunately children with this double handicap do not seem to be a very high percentage of the whole.

It is, of course, much more difficult to evaluate a non-response, but there are observations which can be usefully made even in these circumstances. For example, it should be possible to evaluate the quality of the child's visual and auditory avoidance. The generally blank, non-focused stare of the severely subnormal is very different from the peripheral, eye-sliding gaze of an autistic child. Similarly, the techniques of auditory avoidance are more complex with this kind of child, even though few of them are able to twist the lobes of their ears right into the ear to totally block the stimulus, as did one boy I knew. Both the subnormal and the autistic will put their fingers into their ears, but the subnormal is rarely as skilful in utilising other parts of the body (such as the shoulder), as is the autistic. Even the stereotypies and mannerisms of the truly autistic tend to be more involved and complex, as anyone who has watched one who is a 'spinner' will testify.

There are other possibilities which need to be con-sidered — some have been illustrated by the stories of the chil-dren with which this chapter began. Perhaps the possibility most frequently considered in addition to the question of sub-normality is whether the child is deaf or not. This is more diffi-cult to estimate, and can only be completely resolved over a period of time. It used to be said, rather glibly, that if you rustled a sweet paper behind the ear of a child who was not responding to normal auditory stimuli, you would soon dis-cover if he could hear or not. This is just not so, for it utterly fails to take account of the fact that many of these children are totally disinterested in sweets or, at times, any other kind of food. Even if they do enjoy them but are totally absorbed in, for example, estimating exactly how much force they need to use to set a door gently moving towards closure (which is not an uncommon activity for an autistic child), they will not automatically respond to the sound of a sweet wrapping! It is only when the child will tolerate the head-phones and his audiograms show a consistent pattern that you can really be sure of his degree of hearing. Before this you can establish whether he can hear or not if you arrange for him to be given an auditory stimulus while you carefully watch the pupil of his eye. The pupillar response is an involuntary one and if it can be detected in these conditions then you do at least know that the child can hear — although not to what degree.

So far, in this part of the chapter overall suggestions have been made to illustrate the kind of cues which could help towards a rough diagnosis, but this is not nearly exact enough if the attempt is to be made to give the child maximum help.

Reverting to the children who were described earlier, careful observations on the part of the teacher followed by skilled medical diagnosis established that Sally's problem was basically a medical and not an educational one. The help she needed could only be provided in a hospital. This would inevitably have become obvious in the course of time; but at least she got what help and care could be given to her at an earlier stage.

Once their physical problems had been positively established in the same way the only correct answer educationally for both Jeffrey and Terry was to transfer them to ESN schools, where the pace and style of the teaching was much more appropriate to their real needs. Although Jamey had proved to be minimally brain-damaged and to have a biochemical disorder he continued to be best placed in the school for disturbed children— for the scatter of his IQ tests showed that in some areas he could function much better than a severely subnormal child ever could. His teaching programme had therefore to be carefully devised to help him overcome his weaknesses as far as possible, while at the same time exploiting his strengths. His speech and his ability to think and talk in a much more consistently appropriate manner showed the most improvement and as these improved, so did his ability to reason. His visuo-motor co-ordination proved to be difficult to improve, but he found it much easier to type than to write, so he was encouraged to use a typewriter whenever possible. The most difficult task of all proved to be the lengthening of his span of attention. In a schoolroom learning situation it never got much beyond ten minutes at a time, in a routine 'job' situation it could be maintained for much longer. The future for Jamey will be a sheltered community life such as is provided in a CARE village, where the teaching he has received will enable him to be able to contribute to the working life of the village and also to meet the social demands of such a way of life.

Ned proved to be an elective mute, who had been unable to cope in any other way with the desperate insecurity, the sudden, dramatic and frequent changes of environment he had experienced during a period of about eighteen months of his early life. These had included the disappearance — to him — of the devoted Chinese 'amah' who had to a large extent been his intimate 'mother figure' while the family had lived abroad, the birth of a younger brother, and his parents' own reaction to their altered way of life. In order to help him, the first immediate task was to build up in him a feeling of stability, security and total acceptance, even in his smelly clothes!

At first he was left relatively untroubled. Fortunately, he was normally interested in food, so he soon responded to gentle encouragement to join in at 'milk and biscuit' time and at lunch time. When this group participation did not prove too threatening he began to show an interest in the children playing with Lego and other constructional materials and when the teacher apparently quite casually one day remarked that 'this set was for him if he wanted it', he accepted it quite calmly, and also her praise at the things he made from it. As soon as he was willingly joining in with more things and also showing that he liked sweets and biscuits, operant conditioning techniques using these as rewards could be used without increasing stress on his part, and this helped to speed his progress. The epic day arrived when it was warm enough to fill the paddling pool — the sight of the other children enjoying the water, at last gave Ned the confidence to take off his smelly clothes and get in with them. When he came out of the water he accepted without question the clean clothes that were offered; but for a week or so longer still had to pull on top of them his old vest! The next major break-through occurred when he began to mouth responses to the speech and questions of the people he knew.

As he became more responsive he was also able to accept more controls and the structuring of his activities by the teacher. He began to have sessions with the speech therapist and later became accepted as rather a 'chatter-box'! Ultimately, he was able to move on to a school for slow learners. It was decided that this would be the best placement for him even though with an IQ of 80 on the WISC he was at the top of the accepted range for such schools, since he was still retarded educationally and much better suited to the smaller class sizes and overall population of such a school.

54

A great deal of Ned's improvement depended upon the fact that the parents were also being visited and encouraged to visit the school. In the course of talking things over with the psychiatrist and the teachers the father spontaneously decided to change his job, which paid well but was very demanding of his time and energy, for another, less well paid, which allowed him much more freedom to be at home with his family. Previously his main objective had been to earn sufficient money as fast as possible to buy a house and achieve some measure of financial stability. Later he opted for achieving this more slowly in favour of providing his wife and children with emotional stability. He became rather touchingly proud when he saw Ned openly modelling himself on him, even to the extent of copying his mannerisms. Ned's mother, who had been extremely depressed when we first met her, gradually became less so when she found she had interested people to talk things over with, and she was delighted when her husband made the decision to change jobs.

I have told Ned's story at some length since it illustrates many of the different factors which were involved in first trying to understand the 'why' of his disturbance, and then in helping to resolve it. They included his history, his temperament, getting to know and utilise his interests, assessing his motivations and ability to respond to 'rewards' and perhaps, most importantly, his whole family situation.

These same factors were also involved in helping Jenny and Lucy, but since they were very different as individuals both from each other and from Ned, different techniques had to be used. Jenny, who had learnt to identify with adults since, at home, she had no one else to associate with, and was far too disturbed to play on any kind of equal terms with the neighbouring children, had to be helped to accept and enjoy her childhood. She also proved to have a definite speech handicap which could be helped by intensive individual speech therapy. Both she and Lucy, however, had also been using their speech and feeding difficulties as 'controlling' mechanisms although in different ways. Once a long period of observation and of eliminating other possibilities had made us fairly confident that this was the cause of Lucy's persistent echolalia which was proving so destructive to all her relationships at home and at

55

school, the decision was taken to 'fight fire with fire'. Her echolalia was met with echolalia. She became very angry, but also, in a sense, very active for the first time, and the 'breakthrough' occurred when she suddenly stamped with rage, shouting 'will you remember once is enough to say anything!'

The problems involved in helping Jill will be described in another chapter.

Summary

In this chapter eight children, all originally diagnosed as autistic are described. Recorded observations of the children in the classroom situation, subsequently referred to the relevant specialists, led to a more explicit diagnosis being arrived at for each of these children. Some guidance as to how to make these observations is offered to the teacher. The later history of the children is briefly outlined.

References

1 L. Kanner, 'Early infantile autism' in *Child Psychiatry*, C. C. Thomas, Springfield, Illinois, third edition, 1944.
2 M. Creak *et al.*, 'Schizophrenic syndrome in children', *Br. Med. Journal*, 2, 1961, pp. 889–90.

4 The teacher, the parents and the environment

**BARBARA FURNEAUX AND
BRIAN ROBERTS**

In the previous chapters of this book the questions of aetiology, diagnostic criteria and the identification both of the children in need and of their own particular needs have been discussed. In this chapter and those that follow the question of how these needs can be met will be considered.

Professor Michael Rutter writing in 1967 stated:[1]

> In our present state of knowledge education probably constitutes the most important aspect of treatment and it is to school in one form or another that we must look for the greatest hope of bringing about achievement in the autistic child.

Rosalind C. Oppenheim in 1974 makes exactly the same point when she says:[2]

> No cure has yet been found for early childhood autism. In the absence of a cure appropriate remedial education with its promise of an improved level of functioning and the diminution of bizarre and abnormal behaviour, together with the hope that autistic children so taught will be able to lead meaningful, even if perhaps sheltered, lives in adulthood—remedial education appears the only viable alternative.

This view may well be disputed by those who still feel that education and therapy must be separated and that children with such a severe handicapping condition are in need of some form of therapy. Nevertheless even those who hold this extreme view accept the children's right to some form of education as and when they deem it to be appropriate. The question that will be discussed in this chapter is how it should be provided.

The education of these children is still relatively new, and since, as has already been demonstrated, there is a wide range of opinion as to which children can correctly be regarded as falling into this diagnostic category, it follows that many different opinions exist as to what is the proper way to provide this education; opinions range from the totally structured to the relatively free and permissive. The rationale behind these varying approaches will not be discussed here since it is dealt with in other chapters of this book. Here we shall discuss the essentials of every kind of education, i.e. (1) the teachers, (2) the schools, and (3) the relationships and links between the parents and the homes, and the teachers and the schools.

(1) The teachers

Teachers working in the field of special education, no matter what the handicap of the children in their care, must have certain objectives. First, they must try to achieve as much as possible of the normal academic and social aims of all educational processes; second, they have to attempt to help the children and their parents to come to a realistic acceptance of the handicap and whatever limitations it may impose; and third, they must try to define and meet the special needs of each individual child. In addition, and possibly this is especially true of teachers of the most severely afflicted, they are faced with the need to accept the greater knowledge of themselves that such work almost inevitably brings. They will be forced constantly to examine their reactions and to question their motivations. Not every teacher wishes to do this, and it is not unreasonable that this should be the case. The personality of the teacher is, therefore, as important as his/her professional expertise.

Teacher's personality

It is very interesting to discover when reading the literature, and in discussion with people who are personally knowledgeable on the subject, that, whatever their ideological approach to the education of these children, a great number of 'teacher qualities' are commonly agreed to be desirable. It is felt that these teachers must be kind, warm and accepting and have the ability to project a stable and calm personality—but that they must also be capable of presenting an equally calm, but firm and determined 'front' *vis-à-vis* the child, a 'front' which must be maintained and persisted with in the face of the child's negativism-tantrums and other ways of displayed resistance or apparent rejection of the teacher and all she is attempting to do with and for the child. Apropos of this it is also necessary for the teachers at such a time to appreciate how much easier this is for them than it is for the parents faced with similar be-haviours. It is, or should be, far less difficult when you are not linked to the child by the close and emotional relationship of parenthood. The importance of the teacher realising this will be returned to later in this chapter. She (or he) must be capable of being consistent in her approach when consistency is necessary with an individual child, but also flexible in assess-ing and dealing with the needs of separate children. She must also be able to develop the ability to detect when changes in the child mean that she must alter her behaviour to the child appropriately. C. B. Ferster makes this same point when he says 'in effect the children teach us how to teach them as the changes in their behaviour differentially reinforce our behaviour'.[3]

In our opinion it cannot be stressed too frequently that the condition of the autistic child is not static, nor are they a homogeneous group; therefore, given the above basic qualities, teachers with many different personalities can all deal successfully with these children; indeed it could well be argued that teachers of different personalities are needed at different stages of the child's development.

This can be illustrated if we consider three children, all con-forming diagnostically to the classical Kanner syndrome:

1   John, aged 5, admitted to his special school three weeks previously. On admission he was not toilet-trained and was un-interested in eating or drinking, accepting only well 'mashed' food from a spoon held by an adult who was willing to allow him to continue his absorption in 'spinning' whatever object came to hand while he was being fed; and refusing either by dashing it away, or by consistently closing his mouth firmly while turning his head away, any drink offered to him in any-thing other than his own 'drinking-cup'. He had no speech and

no wish to do anything other than sit on the floor of his class-room 'spinning' or rocking. The only spontaneous change occurred when music was being played — then he would fleet-ingly look in the direction of the music and stop spinning while his rocking took on the rhythm of the music.

2   Anne, aged $7\frac{1}{2}$, who had been in the school for about eighteen months. In that time Anne had become much more aware of other people and accepting of them; she was becom-ing willing to sit in 'groups' and to join in with simple group activities. Her speech was developing and at times she would obsessionally demand 'Waz-zat?' (what is that?) as she picked up or pointed to everything in sight. From being a practical non-eater she had begun to eat willingly and to feed herself but only at this stage with a highly selective and very restricted diet. She had become toilet-trained. However, she was still very negativistic and resisted in every possible way the intro-duction of anything new or the teacher's decision as to what she was required to do. She resorted to violent tantrums at times — but at others simply became totally passive. Her teacher had to persist in her demands in the face of all this but she had also to remember how tenuous Anne's relationship with her and with everyone else still was and judge very pre-cisely exactly which demands she should make and to what degree she could persist in making them and when to relax and allow Anne to do so as well.

3   Simon, aged $11\frac{1}{2}$. After three and a half years in the school, Simon in many ways had surmounted all the main hurdles. He was able to be a member of a remedial class where the major part of the day could be spent on academic subjects. He could talk — had become almost a compulsive eater and was fully able to care for himself personally. However, in many ways he was still totally self-centred and self-motivated. At times, especially if he was interested in the subject being taught, he would work with great attention and persistence; at others he would use every delaying tactic he could think of to prevent himself from having to embark upon a subject he was unwilling to do at that time. The greatest problems sometimes arose when it was necessary to move on from one subject to another. This often used to lead to disturbed be-haviour — sometimes shown in disruptive activities — sometimes

in a determined effort to engage the teacher in a wordy discussion both as to why he had to change and why he could not continue with the thing he was enjoying. His arguments at times could be highly ingenious! He found it most difficult of all to accept the need to stop using something because it was another child's turn to use it. Similarly he could not in the least realise why if, for instance, only one roast potato was left and more than one child wanted it, it was not his automatic right to have it.

Each of these children displayed in different ways and to different degrees problems of similar origins — nevertheless they required very different responses from the teacher working with them. John needed much more gentle 'coaxing' with the teacher able to accept the unpleasant aspects of dealing with a child of 5 who needed all the physical care of an infant. Anne required the utmost care and perception from a teacher who knew when to give and when to demand and who could stand without exasperation the absolute need to respond to Anne's persistent 'Waz-zat?', recognising that this was a genuine wish to know and also that Anne had to be told 'Waz-zat' over and over again about the same thing.

Simon's teacher had to be capable of almost unrelenting firmness and determination and yet be skilful enough to know how to use constructively those aspects of his behaviour (e.g. his persistence) which would otherwise have proved destructive.

As there was a common thread running through the problems posed by the children so the teachers needed the same basic qualities which could be displayed by very different personalities. It would be unreasonable, although fortunately not totally impossible, to expect one person to display all the qualities needed.

There is one other factor which appears to be absolutely crucial — and that is that any teacher attempting to do this work must do so with confidence and belief — both in himself and in the child. They must be so personally secure that they can both show the child their anger or displeasure and also their willingness to freely admit and accept that they have made a mistake. They should not feel that the most important thing is to be 'liked' by the child and distort their own behaviour and responses accordingly. It seems to be of equal importance that they should honestly believe that the child can be helped and improved. The importance of 'teacher expectation' upon results has been experimentally demonstrated, and this factor is no less valid when dealing with this particular group of children. A teacher who does not believe in the possibility that they can be improved has a totally depressing effect on the children and the results achieved and therefore should not engage in this particular form of teaching.

Professional skills

In addition to these qualities of personality it is now generally accepted that the teacher needs to be a skilful teacher and preferably one who has had successful experience at working with normal children. Fortunately it is slowly becoming accepted that the handicapped child does not need a patient, undemanding and not necessarily skilful teacher but rather one who is prepared to use a highly professional approach. It should be axiomatic that 'the less able the child, for one reason or another, the more able and skilled the teacher should be.' In working with autistic children or those children described as having 'autistic tendencies' (a somewhat ambiguous statement) most teaching skills will be needed since the teachers will have to cope with all levels of achievement as the child develops from virtually no display of personality and learning ability to — at the optimum — a full range of these.

Teacher skills

Initially they will need the skills of a good infant teacher, but one who is able to adapt infant methods and apparatus to children who are physically at times more mature than those for whom the apparatus was intended and who may at the same time initially have to be taught through the nearer sensory channels (i.e. touch and smell) rather than the more commonly used distance perceptors of sight and hearing.

As the children progress they will need all the ingenuity and skill of a good remedial teacher of primary school children and finally those of a secondary school teacher. There will be odd inconsistencies and 'overlaps' to be considered because one child at any one time may well be at different stages of maturation with his physical development well outpacing his emotional, social and intellectual levels, or there may be odd combinations of these levels of maturation in the child. These factors will have to be considered when deciding their correct group placement within a school or unit.

Special skills

The teacher who in addition to his basic training also has some special skill or gift can be exceptionally valuable in a school or unit for autistic children as for example a music specialist, a teacher of arts and crafts, a teacher who is willing and able to teach the children to cook and a physical training teacher. Some of the reasons why are briefly described below.

Music. It is a common observation that the majority of these children respond to music. Many mothers make this discovery pre-school and report that they have found the only way to pacify their child consistently has been to play records for him. Many have said that the children respond best to light classical music and least well to 'pop' music — particularly where this is characterised by a dominant loud 'beat'; however, this is not always the case. There are a few children who react violently and hostilely to the sound of music, actually screaming, stamping and covering their ears with their hands. However, it has been noticed that even while doing this, and apparently rejecting the music, they are often swaying to its rhythm or more frequently turning their head from side to side in time to the music. We have found that if you reduce the volume but persist in playing the music, at the same time sitting next to the child or holding him loosely and at the appropriate moment when his noisy reaction has diminished, gently remove his hands from his ears and hold them, even these children relax to the music often ultimately sufficiently to be calmed by it.

The fact that the children are so responsive to music can be utilised educationally in many ways — some of which will be discussed more fully in a later chapter in the book. It can be used therapeutically, to help in speech and language development, to capture the child's attention, as a reward, and as an aid to socialisation.

Arts and crafts. This again is an extremely useful skill for the teacher to possess. With the older children pottery, art work and woodwork have great therapeutic value and also allow the children to 'discharge' much of their emotional stress in a constructive way and one which is more socially acceptable at times. To give some extreme examples:

1 It has proved perfectly possible to transfer a child's interest in 'smearing' and playing with faeces to modelling in clay and plasticine.

2 A child who in angry frustration is banging his own head violently or fiercely rocking a chair can be directed into 'hammering' wooden pegs through a board or nails into wood and this can be developed into a constructive exercise.

3 There is a lot of physical and tension 'release' involved in finger painting; in fact, with many of the children who are seriously inhibited and unwilling to be physically involved it is sometimes an essential activity.

4 The making and then using of puppets and masks enables some of the children to express themselves and their emotions much more freely than they can do in their own personae.

5 With the younger children even obsessive paper-tearing can be developed constructively by an inventive teacher.

These and many other similar activities not only have immediate value but can also play their part in developing responsiveness, motivation, socialisation and language.

Cookery. Many of the above observations apply equally to cooking. The child can be acceptably 'messy', discharge aggression and at the end be rewarded with something to eat! Again educationally cookery has wider applications; there are the obvious ones of developing knowledge of weighing and measuring, and of the cookery process itself. Recipes can be written out and a meaningful discussion can be developed which will help to increase language. Very often the child first

64

learns to 'give' by offering one of his cakes to somebody else and the cookery session can lead to many socialisation exercises. In addition, of course, the children are learning about the use of many things including gas and electricity which will be part of their everyday life. They are also developing concepts of e.g. 'hot', 'warm', 'cold', 'sticky', etc. A cake or biscuit is no longer just something thought of and known as a finished product, the child gradually appreciates it is a compound of its various ingredients and how it is possible to vary the colour and taste by different choice of ingredients. The possible teaching developments are many and are all related to a practical and meaningful context.

Physical education. This has many additional applications to the treatment of autistic children apart from the general and normally accepted aims. It is very rewarding and interesting to see the children's pleasure in their own achievements and to see a totally fearful and withdrawn child gradually developing bodily poise and confidence. It also helps the children to learn to take turns, to join in games and to play ball, etc. The trampoline seems to have a great appeal to nearly all of the children. We also include in our physical training the use of roller skates, bicycles, etc. Many children seem to display their first real freedom of movement on the skates and we have been interested and surprised to note how very few appear to show any anxiety when first putting the skates on and how quickly they both master the art and confidently use it.

It is not possible in this chapter to develop further the uses and values of these and other special teaching skills but one further point should be made, that even with autistic children the teacher's enjoyment of anything he is teaching is a very important factor.

To sum up, it seems possible that any skilled teacher, who *wishes* to work with these children and who has the right personal qualities can do so, provided that his own special training and abilities are used with the right children at the correct stage of their development, and provided that he is willing to read, or to learn from an experienced teacher or other specialist adviser, about the particular problems and handicaps of

65

children falling within this diagnostic category. Ideally he should also be given the opportunity of secondment to a relevant University Diploma Course at some stage of his career — preferably after having had working experience with the children.

(2) The schools

There are many questions to be considered when the decision is made to provide special educational facilities for autistic children and children with autistic tendencies. They will include some relating to the location and type of provision to be made, for example, should it consist of a separate school or unit, or be a special class within an existing school? If the latter, in what sort of school? If a separate school is decided upon, should it be day, boarding or a combination of both? How large should the school be, and what age range should it cover? Questions of organisation will also need to be considered such as the ratio of staff to pupils, and a decision will need to be made as to whether the provision should be for autistic children only or whether it should also cater for children with different handicaps. These topics will be discussed later in this chapter.

The questions above are general ones which relate directly to the particular problem but within each authority there are other local factors which must influence the decisions made. The right provision for a largely rural authority where the population density is low and dispersed must be different from that which is suitable for a densely populated area. This factor may even vary within a large authority.

The overall number of autistic children is not large even allowing for the most inclusive use of the term, and also for the fact that it is, at present, mainly a statistical artefact. As pointed out in chapter 1 it is considered to be of the order of approximately one in every 2,000 schoolchildren — 4·5:10,000 educed in the Lotter survey — and therefore it is very unlikely that there will be more than one or two children in a rural area.

However, this is not invariably true, and it may be that when provision is available more cases will be found, for example when a special unit was set up in Whitstable no less than eight cases were found within a radius of fifteen miles from the centre. The financial aspects cannot be overlooked especially in the present economic climate. The high staff/pupil ratio considered to be essential is a major item in the overall cost, but, in addition there are many other expensive items to be considered which cost relatively little in a normal school, e.g. the cost of providing transport and possibly an escort, all of which must be borne by the authority.

It is obvious, therefore, that there is not, and cannot be, one answer to each of the questions posed in the beginning of this section. Some answers must be largely influenced by practical and financial considerations, others are a matter of opinion and the points that are to be made in the rest of this section should not be taken, therefore, as other than ones for discussion and consideration.

Location of school or class

In deciding upon the location of the provision to be made it is sometimes useful to consider the ultimate aim of project. In this particular case it might be stated as follows:

It is to help the children to function at the highest possible level according to their capacity and also, wherever possible, to enable them to live within the community as a socially acceptable, contributing member of that community. If this is accepted it follows logically that the school or class should be reasonably close to the children's normal home environment. This would provide the maximum opportunity for a very important, indeed essential, part of their education, which is to learn by constant practical experience how to live within the community and to cope with its demands. A child from a rural or village community whose family intended to continue to live in such an environment may be seriously at a disadvantage in after-school life if he has been sent during his school life to a school placed in a totally different setting. The same is equally true of a town child sent to a school in a remote or rural community.

There are two further factors which have relevance in deciding upon the location of the school. The first is the necessity

67

for these children to have the opportunity when appropriate to associate with children who are developing and behaving in the accepted normal manner, for they need child models and stimulus as well as adult interaction and instruction. The second is the need to consider what is the best way to preserve both the family of the autistic child and also his place within the family. Unfortunately it is frequently the case that a family, temporarily relieved of the strain of living with an autistic child, appreciates for the first time the full extent of the burden and finds intolerable the thought of taking it up again. It seems that this is less likely to happen if, somehow, a pattern of 'built-in' relief and support can be established and this may be part of the function of the school.

Day or boarding

Both practical considerations and the points raised above have some relevance in certain circumstances in deciding whether a day or boarding school placement is more appropriate to the needs of the child and his parents. Each offers certain advantages and disadvantages, some of which are very similar to those applying when the same decision is made with regard to children with other types of problems. The obvious particular advantages of a boarding school for these children are two-fold. First, it does mean that the children can have totally consistent planned handling throughout the day, for it would be implicit in the design of such a school that the whole staff, whether teaching or care staff, would work to an agreed programme for each separate child. Second, it would give the families of the children the maximum possible relief. Some of the disadvantages have already been discussed in part, namely the separation of the child from his family and his environment and the possible consequences of this separation.

There are others: first it reduces considerably the opportunities for co-operation and consultation between the school and the parents of the children. Second, the child is compelled by these circumstances to live in two totally separate environments and to relate fairly intimately to two sets of people. The need to adapt from one to the other could present extreme difficulties to the autistic child who is characterised both by his difficulty in forming relationships and by an almost obsessive desire for the preservation of sameness in his environment. Third, a boarding school can have a depressing or detrimental effect upon the staff, particuarly those who are resident.

Assuming equality of provision and teaching, the advantages of day provision are the converse of the disadvantages of boarding provision. Similarly the disadvantages are the converse of the advantages of a boarding school. Consistency of handling can only be totally ensured for the relatively few hours of the week when the child is in school and the parents are given much less relief from the care of their child. They are, however, in a much better position to be able to discuss the child fully with the other people in intimate daily contact with him. There are two possible half-way solutions, namely, weekly boarding or the provision of some beds in a day school. Of the two, the day school with beds seems to offer the most positive advantages. The only advantage of weekly boarding is that it ensures the frequent contact of the child with his home and the opportunity for the staff to be free at the weekends. The advantage to the child and the parents is considerably reduced by the fact that the parents find the weekends when they have total care of the children the most difficult of all to cope with. A day school with beds would offer all the advantages of boarding as and when appropriate or necessary, in a situation that was known and familiar to the child and his family. It could offer relief in all times of stress or illness within the family and could also enable the parents and other children in the family to have normal social intercourse, including holidays, without the disadvantages and embarrassments that frequently arise from the presence of the handicapped child. This should even extend to overnight stays so that, for example, the parents could plan a night out, without being faced with the well-nigh impossible task of finding a babysitter able and willing to cope with an autistic child, or the brother and sisters could have a party with their school friends without anxiety.

Size of school and types of children it is to provide for

These two topics are being considered together since the one

69

has a direct bearing upon the other. In no circumstances can such a school be a large one. The incidence alone would prevent this apart from all the psychological considerations. If it is to be purely for autistic children and children with autistic tendencies it could have the advantage that the children attending it had common problems. Therefore, in theory, the teaching techniques to be used could have some uniformity. In fact, this can only be true to a very limited degree. The terms 'autistic tendencies' and even 'autistic' are so widely and differently used that it is not infrequent to find children with, for example, known brain damage, biochemical disorders, hearing loss, all included within this category. Each of these handicaps requires different teaching methods, which minimises the advantage of confining the school to children in what appears to be, but commonly no longer is, one diagnostic category. In addition the children do not all fall within the same IQ range; as far as the present evidence indicates there are some to be found throughout the spectrum, even though the number found at the higher end is small.

Although the point has already been made it is so important that it is worth reiterating that these children, although they have symptoms in common, are not a homogeneous group.

If in view of this the decision is made to broaden the category of children for whom the school is designed by the inclusion of seriously disturbed and underfunctioning, but not severely mentally retarded children, the school can be larger and provide for more children with one area. This has practical and economic advantages; it also tends to reduce the strain upon the teachers, for there is the possibility in this set-up of more immediate 'teacher-rewards' in the terms of success and of 'feed-back' from the children. The disturbed children with all their problems and difficulties do play and communicate verbally on the whole. They, therefore, provide the essential 'models' for the autistic children. There is evidence that the 'mixture' can be therapeutic but, in certain circumstances, it could also be disruptive and disturbing, particularly perhaps if the teachers concerned were unwilling or unable to cope with both kinds of children. Parents also react differently to the idea, some rejecting it for their disturbed children in case they 'copy the mannerisms of the autistic children', others finding it beneficial to them since it helps them to accept more easily their own children's difficulties in comparison with the much severer problems faced by the autistic child and his parents.

A larger school has organisational advantages. First, it enables progression from group to group to take place within the school. This not only presents the children with immediate aims and objectives but accustoms them to the idea of moving on.

Second, it means a larger staff. This accustoms the children to interacting with more people and gives the staff better opportunities for discussion and communication among themselves. In addition it means that there is better scope for using their individual talents to maximum advantage.

Age of children

There is as yet no agreed policy with regard to special schools as to whether they should be 'all-age' schools or follow the practice of normal schools. With the very disturbed and autistic children there are sound arguments both for an early age of admission (i.e. age $2\frac{1}{2}$ to 3) as with the deaf child, and for an 'all-age' school. Early admission ensures that the child is in an environment which offers education to him as soon as he is able to benefit from it, and it also means that the parents are getting support and daily relief at the earliest practicable time. The effect of this on their tolerance of the child and the family's ability to survive may be very considerable.

The 'all-age' provision, that is with the possibility of staying in the one school from the age of 3 up to 18, does take account of some of the most important of the child's handicaps and allows far more flexibility of transfer. It would mean that the child is transferred to another school purely in terms of his readiness for the move, and not because he has reached a certain chronological age.

Special classes

An alternative way of providing education for these children is by setting up special classes. These classes can either be separate and self-contained or part of a larger school.

71

The separate special classes give the teachers-in-charge freedom to plan their own programme. They are small and therefore intimate in character and should enable the teachers and parents of the children attending to work together very closely. However, they do suffer from all the disadvantages of a small group. The teacher can be very cut off from professional companionship. The children are not presented with the opportunities for progression and wider relationships enjoyed by those in schools. This could tend to reinforce certain of their innate difficulties for there is no need in this situation to develop other than a few relationships nor to accept the need for changes in environment. The whole thing can (and, unfortunately, it is not unknown for this to happen) become totally static with one teacher and perhaps a helper in the same place with the same group of children for years on end. The separate class in a larger school should in theory help to prevent many of these difficulties. These classes are frequently housed in a school for ESN (M) or ESN (S) children. Their success or otherwise seems largely to be determined by the tolerance, acceptance and understanding of the school staff and particularly the Head. The teacher of the class, although in charge of the special class, is also a member of the staff of the school and responsible to the Head of that school. She cannot have complete freedom, since the needs and overall philosophy of the rest of the school must be considered. It is also frequently incorrect to believe that physical closeness ensures integration and acceptance. All too often it leads to irritation and an exacerbation of the problems and differences, particularly when, as in the case of the autistic children and the ESN children, there are necessarily differences in the provisions made and the teaching techniques to be used. One simple example will highlight this, and that is the accepted differences in pupil/teacher ratio for the two categories. It does not need much imagination or experience to see the difficulties this could create within the staff room if tolerances were strained in other ways.

Classroom design

As with the decisions regarding the school provision this is likely to be determined by two main factors, (1) the practical and economic possibilities and (2) the theoretical approach of the teacher. If all the teacher has at her disposal is a classroom in a not particularly modern school, her scope for planning is obviously far more limited than that of a teacher fortunate enough to be working in less restricted or constricting conditions. However, she does have one advantage, and that is the number of children she will be teaching in that classroom will be far fewer than those in any normal class. This will allow her to create the different 'zones' within the room which are suggested to be desirable. The use to be made of the 'zones' will vary to a certain degree according to the ages and stages of development of the children with the group and the amount of assistance which the teacher has. The theoretical approach of the teacher will also play a part in this since this will determine, for example, the amount of materials, visual displays, etc., that are normally on view. Some may believe that these should be kept to the absolute minimum and presented singly in a way totally decided and controlled by the teacher. Others will hold the directly opposite opinion, namely that is preferable to have a wide variety of material available and to take note of anything which the child uses and approaches spontaneously. These observations are then used by the teacher to widen and direct constructively the child's chosen activities. We take the view that both methods have points in their favour and that both techniques have a part to play at different stages of the child's development. Others feel differently and it seems to us that provided it can be shown that the child is benefiting, a teacher will work best if she or he is using the techniques that they believe to be most appropriate. This point of view does indicate the need for the teacher to be constantly evaluating and assessing her work and of ensuring that this is being done also by some other person, e.g. the psychologist. The topic will be returned to and fully discussed in a later chapter.

The essential zones or areas required are roughly the same for the children whatever their age; the size of the area devoted to each purpose will, however, vary as the children get older. Perhaps at this point it should be stressed again that all that is being discussed here is a possible way of designing a classroom. It is certainly not being put forward as the only correct plan. The basic zoning is that commonly found in most modern infant classrooms namely, an area where such activities as water play, sand play, arts and crafts and possibly cooking can take place, an area where actual teaching can be carried out and a quiet 'comfy' corner where the children can relax, listen to music, talk about their 'daily news', listen to rhymes and stories (if this is at all possible) and practise social behaviour, e.g. at milk-times or after cookery. With autistic children there is another important area necessary and that is one for 'time-out'. This is a technique which has been demonstrated to be extremely effective in nearly every school or unit working with these children. Basically it consists of the immediate removal from a group or activity of a child who is disrupting the group, or challenging the teacher's direction by means of temper tantrums, self-attack and other negativistic behaviour. The child is either left alone or supervised, but not interacted with, by the teacher. He is allowed to rejoin the group when this behaviour stops. This area does not have to be large but should be screened at least visually from the rest of the group. Ideally, of course, it is better if it is outside the actual classroom but there are many reasons why this cannot always be arranged and it is not essential.

(3) Home and school relationships

In all branches of education there is a growing tendency to encourage and welcome parent participation within the school. Where autistic children are concerned it is commonly felt that it is equally important that those dealing with them in the school should have knowledge of them in their homes. It is true that there are still some therapists such as Bruno Bettelheim[4] who hold the extreme view that an autistic child can only be helped if he is taken into the treatment situation and the parents rigidly excluded from it. Others also advocate taking the child into a residential placement but making provision within that situation for the parents to stay in also as and when it is felt to be desirable. Some, such as Deslauriers,[5] feel that in order to treat the child it is absolutely essential to evaluate the child's total environment from the child's point of view, and then to help the parents to develop and utilise 'their own alertness and responsivity to the child's communications and cues or messages'. He and his colleagues also believe that the parents have to be included as co-therapists and allies and to be shown, as they wished to know, 'what needed to be done and in what way they could do it'.

Since the child is part of his family his problems are also inevitably family problems and it does not seem either sensible or desirable to decide to treat the child as something apart from his family. There are certain built-in difficulties here since there is conflicting research evidence as to the adequacy of the parents — some researchers claim that their results show that they do not differ significantly from the norm, others that the families of autistic children tend to be inadequate in central drive as compared to other sub-groups (e.g. brain damaged) and more prone to marital difficulties, etc. This is not regarded as an aetiological factor, but much more as a product of the fact that living with an autistic child causes great family stress and this in turn can result in the family becoming dispirited, depressed and divided and abrasive in their approach not only to the child but also towards each other. Deslauriers in the chapter already referred to points out the heart-searching and feelings of guilt which the parents frequently experience and struggle to come to terms with. He also stresses the need to help them to accept that the 'anxiety they had in not being able to cope with their autistic infant was normal; they were baffled and puzzled as everybody is by such a child.' The removing of the child would do nothing to help the parents in this respect. Working with them as well as the child would seem to offer much more positive advantages. We would suggest, however, that the gain from this is not totally one-sided; the school and the other advisers involved can offer professional knowledge and assistance but the parents have to offer on their part an intimate knowledge of the child. Before discussing practical ways in which one can hope to achieve this co-operation it is important to state again a point that was made earlier, namely that the teacher must always try to understand exactly what the strains and stresses imposed upon the parents have been like — and should also attempt to anticipate and discuss with them in advance, their reactions to whatever successes or failures he achieves with the child—understanding why, in some instances, the parents, although disappointed, will find his failures easier to tolerate than his successes. The psychiatrist and other specialists play an important part in this respect, but their role will be discussed fully in another chapter.

Suggested practical measures

The most important thing in developing co-operation is that there is understanding, mutual confidence and acceptance on the part of both the teachers in the school and the parents in the home of the aims and measures being used with regard to the child. This means that there must be a constant interchange of information—communication and discussion are essential. The parents should know about the school and what happens in it, and the teachers, without infringing upon the privacy of the family, should have the opportunity of seeing the child at home and assessing him in this context. It is our firm belief that parents are entitled to full information as to what investigating measures you wish to undertake, why you think they are necessary and what are the findings. They should also know what pressures and demands are being made of the child in school and also what successes or failures are resulting, for example, if the school has succeeded in getting the child to verbalise a request and is then insisting upon it, the parents should both know this and be asked to do the same. This does not mean that the child's life at home should be a rigid continuation of his time in school. He has the right to act differently in the different contexts, but it is important to ensure that there is consistency as far as is possible and desirable in the practice of his hard-won achievements.

The interchange of visits is therefore important and has the added advantage of enabling the child to see his life as a whole and not 'split' into two separate halves, but two interchanging ones with the people in each familiar to and communicating with each other. A most useful and commonly used device is the keeping of a home-school diary with the teacher filling in the news of the child's activities at school and the parent returning it with home 'news'. This has the added effect of again helping the child to comprehend his life as a structured whole as well as developing his conversation in meaningful realistic contexts, for it is a good idea to have a daily group discussion of the interesting bits of 'news' in the children's books.

The parents' visit to the schools can be formal, informal or a mixture of the two, with the informal visits being more of a social activity and a sharing of part of the daily life of the school, and the formal a serious discussion of some aspect of the child's behaviour, progress or apparent lack of it. Similarly with the teacher's visits to the home though here the discussions should probably be carefully monitored in part by the teacher since she should always be aware of the limits her own training should impose, and know when to suggest that the discussion would be more productive if it could be transferred to the school and other specialists, such as, for example, the psychiatrist or the speech therapist involved in it.

Co-operation is also possible and desirable on a practical level—with teachers and parents working together to achieve common objectives, such as the improvement of existing facilities or provision of new ones. This benefits not only the children but also relationships in general. Working together on equal footing for a common aim helps the teachers and the parents to appreciate each other as people not just in their 'roles' towards each other. Many parents also feel far more involved and accepting if it is made clear to them that they have something to give which is of obvious value. It is said 'it is more blessed to give than to receive' and it is not easy to be the one who is forced by circumstances to appear always to be the receiver.

Suggestions for parent participation in the teaching-treatment programme

Many parents enjoy helping their children with their homework and participating in other ways in school activities. When this is the case the child and the school gain also. Some children even begin to learn to read, to write and to count with their mothers before starting school. By the time autistic children reach school age, however, it is unlikely that their parents will even feel that they have learned to cope adequately with their behaviour, nor is it probable that the children will have developed the motivation necessary to learn anything. Very rarely some autistic children show rapid learning ability, albeit in a mechanical fashion, as for example, learning lists of words, with very little comprehension of what they are doing. Normally the effort and strain of containing the child's behaviour is so time-consuming and makes such emotional demands on the parents that they are left with very little time or energy to devote to the needs of any other children in the family, or to each other. Since taking the child out frequently leads to a hazardous or embarrassing experience if the child's behaviour problems attract the attention and critical comments of other people it is not uncommon to find that the family stops going out as a family. This not only produces deprivation, stresses and strains between the members of the family but also limits even further the learning experiences of the handicapped child. It is not surprising therefore to find that the marriage itself is sometimes put at risk, and that the parents can come to feel that a residential placement for their child is the only justifiable solution to their problem. This feeling can only be increased if, as is only too common, even their nights are disturbed and broken because of the poor sleep habits of the child. Many cannot go to sleep easily and remain awake and active until the early hours of the next morning, some are reported to sleep for only a couple of hours a night for years on end. If this is the case at least one of the parents habitually gets little sleep also.

It is obviously highly important to look at ways in which the home situation may be improved. Failing this it may even be the case that any advance made in school is reduced by the responses to the child of bewildered, irritated and demoralised parents. Often ad hoc advice is easily come by from psychologists, psychiatrists, social workers and paediatricians, advice of 'have you tried . . . ?' or 'I would suggest this' variety. Many of these suggestions may well be both sensible and effective but because they are scattered and piecemeal they often have little lasting effect. Often, too, it is difficult for the professional who has no experience of seeing the whole family in the home to envisage the range of problems with which the parents are faced.

The teacher is in a better position to do this, particularly if the need to keep in close contact with the family is, as it should be, accepted as an essential part of her work. A structured home programme drawn up jointly by the teachers and the parents will not only ensure that they are each reinforcing and supporting the gains they are individually achieving but will also enable the parents to see themselves in a new role as equivalent to the teacher in the treatment of their child. This will not only boost their morale, but will also help them to develop fresh expectations for the future, not only of their child but for the whole family. A teacher who gets to know the parents well and who is in constant contact with them by making some home visits is in a much better position to assess what might be done to implement her programme and also be of effective help in the home. She can also determine what changes need to be made, especially in relation to the changes she notes in the child's behaviour at school.

When observing the home circumstances she will note what particular advantages and disadvantages the house provides for carrying out home-based treatments. She will observe the interactions between parents and child, between them and their other children, and other family members. She may usefully note what kinds of household articles exist for promoting interaction and learning situations for the child. Where there are brothers and sisters, she can see how they relate to her pupil; for instance, do they attempt to play with him, help him, ignore him? Do they appear hostile to him, ashamed of him, or are they sympathetic in a realistic way? Such a range of attitudes and responses may well be in evidence at different times. Every household contains resources which may be arranged to help the child in one way or another. Frequently it is difficult for the parents to realise what, and how much, is available for this purpose in their own home, or what can be made or bought at little cost. Similarly, because of the length and intensity of their interactions with their child, it may be difficult for them initially to realise how they might provide the time and energy for participation in a structured programme.

Such a programme needs to be realistically negotiated with them after the total home resources have been evaluated, and

79

perhaps discussed with professional colleagues. What one family can attempt may well be unrealistic for another. It is the teacher's increasing knowledge and understanding of the family circumstances which may provide the most accurate assessment of what is possible. Further, from her daily observation of and work with the child the teacher can assess the grading strategies; what may be an optimum amount of time to work on any one skill or aspect of behaviour, how forceful or insistent one may be without impairing motivation and affecting the relationships.

The clear advantage of approaching the child's problems in this way lies in it being a joint exploration of what is possible and simultaneously it reduces negative emotions and spontaneous reactions which can create a sense of hopelessness. In dealing with the autistic children we are indeed on the frontiers of knowledge.

In addition to the points made above a major consideration is the amount of time the family as a whole and as individuals can devote to carrying out such a programme, for the normal routines of home life must continue, and time must be set aside for the hobbies, interests and leisure activities of each member of the family. Everything must not be sacrificed to the wish to help and improve the handicapped child. It is also important that when the decision as to the amount of time that can be used has been agreed on, it should be kept to, for then the child becomes used to the consistency with which he is treated and this is a very important factor. It is also necessary to decide upon objectives, and to analyse all the steps needed to achieve success in carrying them out. Finally an agreed plan of charting or recording progress is desirable since it can serve both as a reminder and a prompter, and replace subjective impressions with objective reports. The teacher, from her professional knowledge, should be able to advise the parents on both these matters.

A model

The following plan is intended only as an example and a model. It is an idealised presentation and designed to show how any part of the day could be organised without too great a demand being made of any one member of the family. It assumes a family of four—including the autistic child. Each other member of the family works consistently at attempting to modify one aspect of the child's behaviour, e.g. the mother might concentrate on attempting to elicit language for household objects (Task X); the father on developing eye to eye contact (Task Y), and the third member of the family on trying to get the child participating in reciprocating behaviour, e.g. rolling a ball back and forth (Task Z). Figure 4.1 shows how the whole day could be programmed, with each in turn working at their decided task. Obviously such a programme could not, and should not, in fact take place throughout the whole day. Each family would decide how much or how little of it they could guarantee to follow consistently. Even if only a fraction of it can be carried out, the amount of extra treatment hours over a period of a year is considerable and some solid gains can be expected. If they are achieved it will become less necessary to carry out such a formal programme as this.

FIGURE 4.1

A = Father   B = Mother   C = Older sister

Weekends

	Task	Person
9.00 a.m.– 9.15 a.m.	X	A
9.30 a.m.– 9.45 a.m.	Y	B
10.00 a.m.–10.15 a.m.	Z	C
10.30 a.m.–10.45 a.m.	X	A
11.00 a.m.–11.15 a.m.	Y	B
11.30 a.m.–11.45 a.m.	Z	C
12.00 noon–12.15 p.m.	X	A
12.30 p.m.–12.45 p.m.	Y	B
1.00 p.m.– 1.15 p.m.	Z	C
1.30 p.m.– 1.45 p.m.	X	A
2.00 p.m.– 2.15 p.m.	Y	B
2.30 p.m.– 2.45 p.m.	Z	C
3.00 p.m.– 3.15 p.m.	X	A
3.30 p.m.– 3.45 p.m.	Y	B
4.00 p.m.– 4.15 p.m.	Z	C
4.30 p.m.– 4.45 p.m.	X	A

5.00 p.m.– 5.15 p.m.	Y	B
5.30 p.m.– 5.45 p.m.	Z	C
6.00 p.m.– 6.15 p.m.	X	A
6.30 p.m.– 6.45 p.m.	Y	B
7.00 p.m.– 7.15 p.m.	Z	C

Weekdays

Rotate and change to allow for family circumstances. Each person does seven sessions (= 1 hour 45 minutes) per day at weekend, and 30 minutes each during weeknights.

Although there is as yet no evidence about the relative effectiveness of treatment in terms of age at which it is begun, it is often considered that the earlier treatment begins the better. This is perhaps based on a 'common-sense' argument that the longer a child produces autistic behaviour the more self-reinforcing and therefore more difficult to eradicate it becomes. It follows also that the behaviour will be more difficult to replace with appropriate behaviour. If these points are considered substantial, they support the argument for beginning with an intensive programme and lessening it as the child shows progress. The longer he is not learning, both in social and academic respects, the wider the gap which has to be closed, and thus the less the chance he will be admitted to normal schooling. Local authorities should therefore look at the possibility of admitting autistic children to school units prior to ordinary school age (at present the beginning of the term in which the child's fifth birthday falls), if they are to cut the later expense created by high staff-pupil ratios necessary for dealing with this condition effectively.

As suggested earlier, the school or unit can and should serve as a meeting place for parents. A regular conference of parents and teachers to discuss their problems and to get to know each other will greatly increase the effectiveness of the programme and reduce the feeling of isolation often suffered by these parents. Here the parents can examine their individual problems and often help each other in demonstrating for instance how they dealt with a toilet-training problem, eliciting speech, etc. By getting to know each other they might arrange mutual baby-sitting (it is hazardous to leave an autistic child with someone who does not know how to cope with his behaviour), and as a group they can perform many functions. They can act as fund raisers, through jumble sales, etc., for the school; they can organise educating the local community in the problems they deal with, and they might include local colleges and university courses. They might arrange self-help in many ways, including possibilities for holidaying which they had previously not dared to consider. Finally, they may be able to contact parents of children too young to be admitted to the school who are as isolated from help as they themselves previously were.

The National Society for Autistic Children has already done much to put such parents in touch with each other throughout Britain. These parents have not always had a focal meeting place, however, for the low incidence of the condition implies wide distribution. Such meetings, however, may be crucial not only for the morale of the parents, but, as suggested above, for the very effectiveness of the programme itself.

The teacher's role in this may be seen as that of a catalyst. She is not the 'expert' or even necessarily the leader in these events. In this model, parents and teachers may be seen as coming together as co-workers in a vital experiment, developing between them a body of experience and expertise which can act as a model for others in similar circumstances; for instance in schools for and with parents of Downs syndrome children.

The advantages are obvious. A family existence that previously was experienced so negatively is turned into a challenging event which in turn is part of a larger community event, where new friendships are forged and self-help takes on a larger meaning. Such a programme can not only act as a model, but as a training area for professionals.

Appendix: The Linden Bridge—a model

In April of 1977, the Linden Bridge School was opened. It has been purpose-built by Surrey County Council to re-house The Lindens and is designed to meet the needs of severely disturbed and autistic children. A description of it is included as an appendix to this chapter as a model of the sort of provision one local authority is making for these children. There are, of course, many other ways of catering for their needs, so this description is not intended in any way to imply that this is the one and definite way of setting up such a school.

The Linden Bridge School is on a four-acre wooded site in Worcester Park with the Hogsmill River nearby. Many of the trees are preserved so that the character of the site is unaffected as far as possible. The whole perimeter is surrounded by an unobtrusive but effective chain-link fence to ensure the privacy of the school and, more importantly, the safety of the children. The site is not isolated in any way. It is not far from a busy through road, and the immediate neighbourhood is a pleasant housing estate. Buses and trains are all nearby, and there are plenty of shops within walking distance. Both Kingston and Epsom are not too far distant and very easy to get to by public transport. There is, therefore, no difficulty about taking the children out to give them the practical experiences within the community which are considered an essential part of their education. The children have been participating for some years in the 'Riding for the Handicapped' scheme and there is plenty of room within the grounds to develop this activity which has proved very valuable to them all.

The buildings

The main building on the site is the school itself—plus the hostel provision which is being provided—since the school provides some residential places. The teaching areas of the school are all on one level with an enclosed central courtyard. The hostel is two-storey and at one end of the building. The materials used throughout are brick and timber and not concrete modules. At the far end of the site, quite separate from the school and not approached through the grounds, are two teacher houses. The teachers who inhabit them therefore, like all other teaching staff, go in and out of the 'main' gate. This has been a deliberate decision to give them maximum privacy. The houses are, however, linked to the main building by a private internal telephone circuit. One house has been allotted to the Deputy Head, the other to a senior member of the teaching staff.

The accommodation

The school is intended for fifty children at present. There are twenty-five beds available. The classrooms are all large and all face outwards to the grounds. At a later stage it is intended to build a covered terrace outside each room, as an extension to the classroom. There are six main classrooms: two for the very young children, two for the next age group, and two for older children. All classrooms have large 'walk-in' cupboards, and the four for the younger groups have their own built-in toilet and cloakroom accommodation. The facilities for older children are part of the shower block and adjacent to the gymnasium.

All classrooms have water laid on. They are planned so they can be 'zoned'. Those for the younger ones have a relatively large tiled area to allow for sand and water play, painting and all forms of 'messy' activity. The rest of the room is carpeted, and includes a teaching area and a more informal 'cosy corner'. The 'wet' area is much reduced in the rooms for the older children as most of their craft and other activities takes place out of the classroom. Facilities are provided for projection of films, slides, TV, etc. All the rooms are wired to allow for the use of teaching machines. The rooms for the older children are also carpeted and capable of 'zoning' as the teacher wishes and as is appropriate to the needs of the children. There is a separate music room fully equipped, and a gymnasium or 'activity' room which also serves as Assembly Hall and in which a stage can be easily erected. Stage lighting facilities are being built in. A site adjacent to the gymnasium is being earmarked for a swimming pool, and 'Green Shield' stamps and money are being actively collected to make the pool a reality as soon as possible. The shower area will be capable of serving the needs of the pool as well as the gymnasium. A housecraft centre with an outer patio is provided for the older children. This room is again 'zoned'. One area is designed for dressmaking, and there are also facilities in this area for hairdressing and beauty-culture. There is a laundry area, a teaching area, a cooking area where both gas and electric cookers are provided, and an 'entertainment' area, which is regularly used for 'entertainment' and social training. Another craft room is equally comprehensive, and includes facilities for pottery (with a kiln), woodwork, metal-work and an art studio. Both craft rooms are very large as is also the dining room, which can be 'screened' into sections, so that children at different stages of social training can, if necessary, be separated, since they will be expected to conform to very different standards of behaviour according to their state of development. Separate from all these rooms a 'shop' has been set up more or less in the form of a supermarket. This is used as a preliminary training experience prior to taking the children into the real shops outside. It is used by all the children although, of course, the complexity of the training will vary from group to group.

Staff rooms

The staff room, which is fully adequate in size for the number of staff, has kitchenette facilities and staff lockers in addition to the sitting area. Adjacent to it are the Office and Headteacher's room. Looking out on to one end of the central courtyard are two sound-damped rooms — one intended to be used by the speech therapist and educational psychologist, the other for the medical staff and used by the psychiatrist and the school doctor. The audiologist and dentist also use these rooms. Water is laid on in both and sinks and basins provided. They are also fully wired to take equipment, and fitted with mirrors, etc. as needed. Near to the shop and these rooms a part of the circulation area is set up as a parents' and visitors' waiting area.

Residential provision

This is on two floors and combines staff accommodation with children's bedrooms. A sick room and medical room are also included in this section. There is accommodation for senior care staff in the form of three-bedroomed flats and also smaller flatlets for assistant care staff. Similar accommodation is provided for a resident housekeeper, and a gardener-handyman. This staff accommodation can be flexibly used according to the appointments made, for example, married accommodation could be provided if a teacher was married to a member of the care staff, the gardener-handyman to the full-time cook and so on.

The children's accommodation is designed as three 'family groups'. Basically their rooms are one-, two-, or four-bedded, but the two- and four-bedded rooms can be screened off to form separate cubicles if required. All the children's rooms are electrically linked by a modified 'baby call' system to the duty room which is 'manned' throughout the night. It is also strategically sited to control the only flight of stairs which is accessible during the night. The sick room leads off the duty room. There is plentiful toilet, shower and bathroom provision.

All food is prepared and cooked in the school kitchen and there are complete launderette facilities available to all the staff.

Exterior

Brick garages are provided for resident staff, and ample parking for day staff and visitors.

Playing fields are being marked out, as is also the asphalted playground. A site has been set aside for an 'adventure' playground which will be developed as soon as funds are available. In addition, there are the wooded areas, and some gardens will be planned and planted.

Staffing

The teaching staff comprises a Head, a Deputy Head, eight assistant teachers, a music specialist, a domestic science teacher and an arts and crafts master. In addition there are seven welfare assistants to work with the staff in the class and craft rooms, and a clerical assistant.

The school does not close for normal school holidays, but

87

the teachers do have their full holiday allocation, hence at least one teacher at a time is on holiday throughout the year, which is the reason for the number of assistant teachers allowed. The Head and Deputy can never be on holiday at the same time apart from total school closures.

The care staff will eventually consist of two senior members and three assistants.

In addition there is also a resident housekeeper, the cook and her kitchen staff and the gardener-handyman and his cleaning staff.

Some teachers may at times be required to take care of the children after school hours, and the resident teachers are expected to be immediately available (by agreement between themselves) if the care staff are faced with an emergency of any kind which requires their advice or assistance. Similarly, the Headteacher, although not resident, will be available if a situation arises which necessitates her presence.

It is intended that on the one staff, the different members will fulfil different roles in the children's lives, and that each member of the staff will have the time and opportunity to follow their private lives as well as their professional duties.

Professional advisers

A visiting consulting psychiatrist attends for not less than two sessions a week, a school medical officer routinely comes once a month and more frequently if required, and an educational psychologist again comes routinely once a month. In addition there will be a speech therapist and it is hoped that this appointment will be a full-time one. The audiologist and school dentist will continue, as now, to visit, to inspect or check all the children every six months. In addition to this visiting specialist staff, the school is fortunate enough to be allowed to use the full investigatory facilities of Queen Mary's Hospital for Sick Children at Carshalton. This includes the EEG Department and the facilities of the Pathology Laboratories.

Use of beds

Since it is felt that it is essential not to separate the children from their families, and also for the teachers and other members of the staff to know the whole family and not just the child entrusted to their care, the school is a day school but provides some residential places. With the increase in numbers it is inevitable that some of the children will live too far from the school to come in daily. They can therefore be taken as boarders, many of whom, however, return home at weekends as may be agreed between the parents and the school.

Approximately one-third of the beds are always reserved for purposes of family support and relief. They are available to all the parents in times of stress or family illness, or to enable the parents and siblings to have some social life, or even a period free from the strains and constraints imposed by the presence of the handicapped child. The beds can also be used to allow the rest of the family to go on a holiday which would not be beneficial to the handicapped child, and whose presence on the holiday would seriously and adversely affect it.

Transport

The children who mainly come from the county of Surrey but also in part from adjoining boroughs and counties are transported to and from the school by private car hire firms who hold contracts from the county to provide this service. They are picked up from home and returned there in the evening. A school bus or coach is not practicable because the children come from such a wide area. For the same reason public transport cannot be used.

References

1 M. Rutter, 'Schooling and the autistic child', *Special Education*, 56, 1967, 10.2, pp. 19–25.
2 Rosalind C. Oppenheim, *Effective Teaching Methods for Autistic Children*, C. C. Thomas, Springfield, Illinois, 1974, chapter VI, p. 91.
3 C. B. Ferster, 'Positive reinforcement and behavioural details in autistic children', *Child Development*, 32, 1961, pp. 437–56.

4 This extreme view has been modified in his latest book, *A Home for the Heart*, Knopf, New York, 1974.

5 A. Deslauriers and C. Carlson, *Your Child is Asleep: Early Infantile Autism*, Dorsey Press, Homewood, Illinois, 1969, chapter IX, pp. 173 and 169.

5   Working with the younger children

BARBARA FURNEAUX

PART 1

Introduction—Two poems by 'Matthew'

1   *A Lonely Wood*

> I hear owls hooting
> I'll get a bit lonely
> And worried
> The wood is so lonely and it's very quiet.
>
> I feel so sad,
> And it's a wild forest,
> I think there are lions in this forest
> And snakes
> And I keep moving.

2   *A Lonely Bedroom*

> I went to bed and went to sleep,
> I hear noises in the dark,
> And I see shadows which mean
> A ghost is coming in my room.
> I heard my door open
> The hinges squeak,
> I got out of my bed
> And no one was there
> I shut the door
> And I went back to my bed
> And to sleep.

91

These two poems were part of a series written by Matthew between the ages of 10 and 11. Perhaps they are not particularly good poetry for a child of that age, but to me they are fascinating as a clear and spontaneous statement of his inner emotions made by a child who, at $6\frac{1}{2}$, was only ever heard to use three words and then inappropriately, 'broken', 'bye-bye' and 'mummy'. He was also a child who by then had been seen on separate occasions by no less than four different psychiatrists all of whom had diagnosed him as autistic.

One of the last poems in the series is the following:

The Big Giant

> I went out to the wood in the dark
> And I saw a Giant
> He was friendly
> I didn't seem to be frightened of this giant
> He had black hair
> And he had a black long beard
> He was tall like an apple tree
> And he went away
> Thumping his big feet.

Matthew went on to compile an anthology of his favourite poems, showing a marked preference for those of W. H. Davies although he also chose some ballads, such as 'Sir Patrick Spens'. Some of the Davies poems he selected echoed the themes in his own, others are interesting choices for a child of his age and history. For example the poem 'One by One' which begins:

> Few are my friends
> But kind and true
> One by one
> I lose my few.

Others which he chose deal with themes of life and death, and the consciousness of the passing of time.

At the time when Matthew wrote his poems and selected the others he had already been able to move on from a special school for autistic and severely disturbed children to a normal primary school where he settled in successfully. Later he progressed to a secondary school at the appropriate age. He, like Jill, described in chapter 3, was a child who conformed in every way to the classical diagnosis of autism. In this chapter an account will be given of some of the techniques which have been evolved by us to teach such children and which have been found to succeed in some cases, although not always to the same degree or extent.

Analysis of the problem

'It is not surprising, perhaps, that a child who does not speak, who shrieks when baulked, who spends hours in repetitive activity, who is seemingly oblivious to all other beings, and who is nevertheless in excellent health, should, as a result, have two forlorn and bewildered parents. In his first six months Matthew showed no particular abnormality, yet paradoxically, he seemed an unusual baby. Within the third to the sixth month we were straining to reassure ourselves of his normality. He showed himself unresponsive to affection, disliked being handled in any way. In all he was a quiet baby as far as tears and cries were concerned — but — at a cost. From that time and for many years, whenever opportunity availed he rocked and swayed incessantly, rhythmically and far into the night with a seemingly endless concentration of energy. Solitude seemed a prerequisite to Matthew and his need for sleep was uncommonly restricted. Other gross features were added to mutism. There was continuing unresponsiveness and near intolerance to demonstrations of affection. Any such would inevitably lead to a strange squealing cry of distress. Similarly he would turn from a straight glance or stare. Perhaps his stoic behaviour to pain may have been, in part, due to a failure to recognise human aid. But he did have one solace, a hint that his inner world was not unfeeling. It was a pathetic fragment of flannelette dragged on every excursion — dirty, begrimed but clearly lovable. It was always with him, or its loss was signified by loud cries of distress.'

93

This account of Matthew was written by his father, and it indicates all the difficulties that a teacher working with these children may be faced with at the time of their admission to school. They can be summarised as follows:

1. The children appear to have no ability to form emotional relationships.
2. Their only apparent motivation appears to be the preservation of their established behaviour patterns.
3. They do not use full focal vision.
4. They give a bizarre response or alternatively none to sound stimuli.
5. They are apparently unresponsive to pain, even when this is self-inflicted.
6. They commonly have no speech or minimal echolalic speech.
7. They are frequently very difficult to feed and quite unresponsive to proffered sweets or other foods commonly used as 'rewards'.
8. They are often hyper-active, absorbed in a self-determined activity, or, alternatively, practically immobile.
9. They often prove to have a high tolerance for drugs and so are difficult either to sedate by means of drugs, or to be made more manageable by their use.
10. They are frequently at the minimal extreme of the height and weight percentiles for their age, although normally they prove to have no positively established physical or organic damage.

Many of these problems have their effect on the teacher/child interaction. Because of the children's inability to form relationships they are quite unresponsive to the teacher's reaction to their behaviour. Her approval or disapproval, no matter how it is displayed, appears to have no potential for 'rewarding' or 'punishing' them. Similarly because of their lack of interest in food or sweets they cannot be 'rewarded' by means of primary satisfactions. This is not invariably the case; some children are responsive to such 'rewards' and, if this is so, the task of the teacher is easier in consequence. Their insistence on the preservation of sameness in the environment and total absorption in their activities, has just got to be broken into, and this may result in severe 'temper tantrums'. They will have to be encouraged or taught to look and to listen, and every attempt must be made to develop speech and language. The first essential tasks are, therefore, to develop relationships, to initiate responsive behaviour, to develop motivation, to reduce negativism, and to develop some form of communication, leading on, if at all possible, to the development of speech and language.

The early stages ('To see where they are going')

'But never think that you know the answer because you are dealing with an individual who may want to go very different routes which, for him, may be better. That's why I feel more comfortable behind the children so I can see where they are going. . . .'[1]

When dealing with children with such acute difficulties as those described above it is most important first to define your objectives. Ours have already been set out in the preceding section of this chapter. Second, it is necessary to choose by which means you are going to try to achieve them. Initially there is one main choice. Put very simply, either you can choose to compel the child to accept your controls and your choices of 'acceptable' behaviour and 'desirable' activity, or alternatively you can choose to 'lead from behind'. If this is your choice you must first spend a period carefully observing the child, and then subsequently try to develop and utilise constructively the things he is doing spontaneously. In this way they can become positive and productive, instead of being destructive barriers to all attempts to come close to him. The choice of approach is very much a personal one of the teacher's. Whichever one is used the main objectives are the same, and success in the form of improvement in the child has been achieved by both means. Apart from the teacher's own preferences other factors are important. These include (1) the teacher's belief in the chosen technique, and (2) the personality of the child plus the extent of his remoteness. If the child is accessible in any way and if his responses can be either positively or negatively reinforced, then it may well be that the quickest results can be obtained by using the first approach. This is a valuable method, scientifically based, which will be further discussed later in this chapter. If, however, the child is inaccessible there is a limit to what can be achieved by using this approach at this stage of the child's development, and very often the use of it too soon has been shown to have the opposite effect to the desired one. C. R. Ferster states that he has found that 'much of the atavistic behaviour of the autistic child is maintained because of its effect on the listener'.[2] He continues, 'the most fundamental way to eliminate a kind of behaviour from an organism's repertoire is to discontinue the effect the behaviour has on the environment.' It is also the case that often there is no 'carry-over' of the results obtained on any other aspect of the child's behaviour. It is for these reasons that initially we prefer to use the second technique.

The first approaches

The first aim in this method is to learn from the child. It is essential therefore to look for any cues which may be provided by his behaviour. During this first period in our school the child is in a room with other children. There is a controlled overall structure to the day, with periods of individual activity being interspersed with group sessions. These include music, 'cookery', painting, sand and water play and, of course, the normal breaks for meals and toilet-training sessions which are of vital importance at this stage (not least for the benefit of the parents). During the individual teaching periods a wide variety of play material, sensory training apparatus, etc. is available. The teacher takes each child separately to try to interest and involve him in the material. However, since the object is to 'learn from the child' both his acceptance of and withdrawal from the proffered activities are accepted. Some of the children are so completely withdrawn that they appear to be totally uninterested and wish only to spend the time involved in their own ritualistic activities or indulging in their stereotypies: endlessly rocking perhaps, or 'spinning' whatever comes to hand, or absorbed in their own finger and hand movements. If this is the case then this is where the teacher must start. It is possible, with a little ingenuity, to devise ways of developing these activities so that they become something that two people do together. For example, we had one little girl who was absorbed in playing with pieces of chain. All the hand-basins were rapidly denuded of their plugs when she first came, since she wrenched them out of the basins in order to get the chains by which they were attached. Once she had the chain she would watch it closely as she skilfully 'flicked' it, appearing to look how she could vary the pattern of its movement. It was completely non-productive to remove it forcibly in the attempt to turn her attention to something else, since if you did she went rigid with rage, screaming and beating at the ground with her extended foot for as long as the chain was withheld. When, however, the teacher appeared one day wearing a very bright chain with a glittering pendant suspended on it, the child's interest was immediately caught. She even focused her eyes on the teacher momentarily, before withdrawing them to concentrate on the chain again. When she reached out to try to snatch it from the teacher's neck, she tolerated her outstretched hand being held as she saw that the teacher was willingly taking the chain from her neck. Once she had taken it off the teacher removed the pendant and let the child handle the chain freely, but she kept the pendant in view and also held her hand near to the free end of the chain. Several times the child turned away from her absorption in the chain to glance at the teacher and the pendant which obviously attracted her. When she deemed the time to be appropriate, and the chain was still, the teacher made no attempt to take it back but gently threaded the pendant on to it again. At once the child let go of the chain to finger the pendant. Without disturbing this the teacher then picked up the chain and fastened it round the child's neck. She remained very still for a moment then began excitedly to flick both the chain and the pendant, appearing to be delighted with the whole situation. Then, however, in what we had come to regard as a typically autistic reaction, she seemed to become very angry (perhaps because she had momentarily lowered her defences?)—pulled the chain from her neck and threw it down as if rejecting both her former acceptance of it and the teacher's participation. Nevertheless the first approach had been made and accepted. The next few times she took the chain and the pendant much more readily and wore them for longer and longer periods. The time came when it was she who chose to stay close to the teacher, and when one day the teacher began to thread shiny beads she became interested at once and soon took over the activity. Her range was then extended, she would thread beads on to fixed rods, and gradually she attempted a wide range of sensory training apparatus and puzzles of various kinds. At this point it became possible for the teacher to alter the procedure, and to increase the demands she made upon the child. This was reasonable because:

1 The child could now be rewarded by being allowed to play with the chain and the pendant she had come to prefer above all others.
2 She was now interested in the other activities.
3 She was also motivated to do them for the pleasure the activity gave her.
4 She was prepared to respond to the teacher's guidance and direction, to a certain extent.

She therefore began to insist that the other activities should be done before she gave the chain to the child. There were some 'storms' before this was established, in fact the precious chain was snapped in two by the child in one of the 'battles'. Interestingly enough when this happened and the child realised what she had done, her screaming rage turned into some of her first real tears of genuine distress. Fortunately, the chain was easily mended, and we all felt that through this incident the child had taken a further step along the road to normal reactions.

I have described this utilisation and development of a child's obsessive activity at some length as an illustration of our technique. We have found that by using similar stratagems it is possible to develop and utilise nearly every ritualistic activity that the children display. The example also shows how one technique used by the teacher shades into another as it becomes appropriate. There are many other aspects of the children's behaviour which can be exploited. As teachers we tend to use mostly the two sensory channels of sight and hearing; these are the very ones that autistic children tend most commonly to inhibit or appear unable to use in the normal way. The reasons why this is the case are still open to research and debate. From the practical teaching angle this presents great difficulties for there are no ways by which you can compel a child to 'look and listen'. You can certainly demand that he does so and even firmly turn and hold his head in the required direction. But you cannot forcibly hold his visual attention, and even while his head is held, the child's gaze will not usually be focused on you. One strategy is therefore to give the child a reason for wanting to look and listen to you. Many of the children do seem to utilise spontaneously their nearer sensory modalities i.e. smell and touch. Even when they are beginning to use sight and hearing in the normal way they still first smell or feel everything when it comes their way. It is easy to see if this is the case and which is the child's preferred sensory channel. It can then be exploited. If a child is a 'smeller' you can encourage him (or her) to approach you by the use of perfume; similarly if he likes to touch or stroke new materials, you can, by wearing such things as highly polished shoes, fur or other soft trimmings, patterned material or jewellery, attract the child to come close enough to feel the thing that has attracted him. The pleasure this gives him is usually sufficiently rewarding to induce him to repeat the experience. The point about this is that by using these methods you are not forcing yourself upon the child and so perhaps increasing his resistance to whatever it is you wish to do with him, but motivating him to come towards you. For, although in the first place it is the attractive smell or material and not the person wearing it that the child is approaching, once he is near, by increasing his range of stimuli, you can thereby extend and increase the child's awareness of you, as the source of the thing he finds attractive. Once this has been achieved you can widen and develop the child's interests in a similar way to utilising a ritualistic activity. For example, children can learn to identify and then classify a wide range of things from their 'feel' and their 'smell'. Subsequently they do begin to look at the things and also to listen to you naming them, their colour, shape, etc. Again as the child's interests grow the teacher can alter her technique accordingly and increase the demands and pressures she makes and imposes upon the child. The amount of time it takes to reach this stage varies a good deal from child to child. When it takes a long time, for instance six months or more, it can put a great strain on the tolerance of the parents who, not unnaturally, are looking for and hoping for, much quicker signs of progress. This, therefore, is one of the periods when it is most important for there to be frequent communication between the teacher and the parents, and also for the teacher to continue to believe in the validity of the technique. In our experience it does succeed in the majority of cases and does lead on to progress in many directions with a great reduction of, although not elimination of, the number of times when it seems that you have to 'fight' the child to make every advance. If, however, after a reasonably extended period there is no sign that the child is beginning to respond, then it is important to re-assess the situation and to try to consider both the possible reasons why no progress has been made, and also, alternative approaches, and then act accordingly.

'Temper tantrums' and dealing with self-abuse

It is probably true to say that everyone who has been in any form of contact with autistic children has also seen or experienced one of their outbursts of screaming rage. Sometimes it is possible to surmise what has provoked the outburst, but at other times it literally seems to 'come out of the blue'. In these tantrums, the child usually goes rigid and then either shakes or beats at the floor or the furniture, etc. with one extended limb. Alternatively, and this is perhaps the most disturbing of all to the observer, he begins to beat his head hard against the door, wall, the floor, or a pillar or post. At times the sound of the blow is quite sickening. The child is also screaming or making loud crying noises, but there is rarely any sign of a tear. When it is possible to guess the origin of this behaviour it is usually that the child is strenuously resisting an attempt to alter his behaviour. This could include trying to initiate a new activity, such as getting ready for a meal, or trying to remove an object which for some reason he is unwilling to give up, or simply that the teacher has attempted some form of physical contact. Apropos of the latter, we have learned that it is most important to keep offering this to the child by appearing to accept his rejection but then coming back again and again and in such a way that it becomes acceptable to the child. The actual warmth of human contact in both senses of the word, is fundamental to all relationships, and in time is as pleasurable to an autistic child as it is to any other. One of the tragic complications of this particular handicap is, however, the effect its manifestations have on other people, particularly the parents. If a child seems to reject being cuddled, cannot be comforted, is difficult to feed and gives no sign of recognising his parents as different from any other person, in other words appears to reject them and all they have to offer, this is so hurtful that, to shield themselves from further hurt, they cease to offer these things. A child who is already deficient in this sort of response is, in consequence deprived of all the necessary stimulus to develop it. The great strength of the teacher in this situation is that as she does not have the strong emotional link with the child she does not feel the same intense rejection, and so can continue to offer the thing the child so badly needs. If and when the child does respond though it is essential for the teacher not only to remember all this, but also for her to explain it to the parents, so that they are not left in the ambivalent emotional position of having to accept help from a teacher who is getting from their child a response which they could not get.

When a child is having a tantrum as described he very rarely responds to a command to stop it, although occasionally if this can be said in a loud voice before the tantrum has really developed, and if the child is already relating in some way to the person giving the order, it can be aborted. Occasionally too, if the same conditions operate, the well-known device of distracting the child's attention to something else can work. Most commonly though it is necessary to stay close to the child and see the tantrum through. This is not always easy as at times it can last for quite a period. If the episode appears to stem from the child's determination to resist an alteration in his activity or to respond to the teacher's request then it is important to repeat the instruction as soon as the tantrum is over, and to continue to do this until the child complies. The somewhat surprising consequence of this is the frequency with which the child seems to be relieved and pleased that you have persisted in this way and so helped him to a new achievement. These episodes are wearing to the child and the adult alike. We have learnt, therefore, to limit their incidence by only forcing issues with the child when it is necessary to do so if the child is to continue to make progress, and only when a relationship has been established between the child and the teacher. Some of the worst episodes, however, do not appear to have been precipitated by the action of another person but to have been triggered off by something within the child or which is happening at home, or of so little significance to anyone else that it is impossible to identify it. It is often in these episodes that the child will resort to self-abuse in such ways as pulling out handfuls of his own hair (never yours or another child's) or biting his own hand or wrist so fiercely that it can be permanently damaged or scarred. One can only speculate as to the reasons behind this. Sometimes it seems as if the child is in the grip of a strong emotion which he lacks all ability to discharge normally. Other manifestations of this are the occasions when the child is able to show he is very angry and even goes so far as to begin the action of striking the person who has aroused his anger but can never actually hit anyone. The movement is either halted at the moment of impact, or all the force behind it is inhibited and only a very light blow is struck. The child's anger is then still undischarged, and this again can lead to self-attack. In either of these instances it is only possible to hold the child firmly in such a way that he cannot damage himself until the fierceness of the impulse has passed. There are, however, other times when the child does everything he can to draw attention to the attack which he is making upon himself, and then it does seem that this behaviour is being used as a means of controlling the adult. We have recently admitted an unusually articulate little boy with strong autistic tendencies, and who came on the first day with severe facial bruising and a large bump on his forehead. Immediately the teacher tried to interrupt his self-determined activities he banged his head hard on the table, and when this did not appear to affect her, he did it again calling out at the same time, 'I'm banging my head.' The teacher's cool reply, 'It is not hurting me', startled him into stopping. It was not so easily resolved by this one instance but gradually the consistent refusal of everyone to react to this behaviour as he wished them to, reduced it considerably. It is not easy for a teacher or any caring adult to respond in this way to the disturbed behaviour of such an afflicted child—the natural response is to comfort and console, but if this is what is done it often has no effect and tends to reinforce the destructive behaviour of the child. The reference to Ferster already quoted in this chapter makes this same point, and much of the experimental work done by O. L. Lovaas and his team in California showed that self-destructive behaviours are maintained in the autistic child's repertoire because they control the behaviour of those in the child's orbit. In the most extreme cases it is not always sufficient to ignore the child's head-banging and self-abusive behaviour, in fact this can increase the intensity of the attack. Lovaas sometimes used electric shocks to extinguish it, which may seem extreme until one remembers that all other techniques have failed and the child is at risk of doing himself a serious and permanent injury. I have found that it is possible to stop such behaviour by using a technique which could well look alarming to the uninformed observer and could also be open to misinterpretation. It consists of appearing to show that you are prepared to partake in the activity unless the child abandons it, for instance, if he goes to bite one hand you take hold of the other and act as if you are going to do the same, or, if he begins to pull out his hair and bang his head you firmly grasp some more of his hair. The indication that this is your intention, done very positively, has always proved sufficient so far to cause the child to abandon his extreme self-attack. It should be stressed that this technique should only be used if all else has failed and the child is likely to cause himself serious injury. So far in all the years I have been working with autistic children I have only had to use it with three children, but in all three cases it was immediately effective.

Social training

The education of autistic children in the early stages has to cover every aspect of their life. On admission to our school many of them are not toilet-trained, unable to sit and eat a meal normally and in the company of other people, unable to feed themselves or to use table cutlery, unable to travel other than in the security of a private car, impossible to take into shops or restaurants, and quite unaware of the dangers of traffic, or the value or use of money. The achievement of any

103

of these skills makes life that much easier for the child, his parents, and the other people involved in his life. If they can all be acquired the child is well on his way to being acceptable in the community, and to coping with its demands, even if he is still unable to read and write, or even to talk. We therefore give these areas a high priority in our teaching programme. As soon as possible we also begin to attempt to teach the child to try to take account of how his actions affect other people, and also to appreciate how the other person feels. Many handicapped people have to relate everything first to the way it affects them in order to survive in the competitive conditions of everyday life. Autistic children do this to an extreme degree. To a certain degree, we all do the same throughout our lives, but when you are growing up in a world of normal relationships you learn to modify and control this as part of the process of growing up. The nature of the handicap of autistic children means that this process does not start in the normal way and unless it is initiated as part of the educational programme it will not happen spontaneously. The role of the teacher is a very comprehensive one and often involves meeting basically unpleasant demands. For example to tolerate incontinence and to deal with its consequences gets progressively distasteful with the increasing age of the child, yet it is a fundamental necessity and often also involves coping at the same time with fierce resistance and tantrums as already described; because of this many mothers have, not unnaturally, abandoned the effort in favour of preserving some degree of family peace. In school it can never be abandoned until control has been achieved. Apart from all else, such efforts can be boring and frustrating particularly at the stage when the child, having not performed on the pot, does so immediately after he has been redressed and gone back into the classroom! The actual training is basically the same as that used with babies, with the teacher or whichever member of staff is training that particular child remaining with him throughout, and no matter how little response she gets from the child, verbally encouraging, praising, or scolding as is appropriate.

Meal times and lunch breaks also involve continuous repetitive training. Many of the children cannot drink from a cup or will only drink from one particular cup (something that can be tolerated in the early stages but must be modified later) and will only accept one particular drink. Similarly in terms of eating some of the children wish to keep to a very restricted diet (fish fingers and chips in the case of one boy for example, and very fat bacon and mushrooms in the case of one girl). Others are quite unused to sitting and eating from a plate of their own and expect to take off the plates of the other children the things they wish to eat. To a certain extent the other children deal with this and help to stop it, but it is still necessary to train the child to eat from a plate of his own. Nearly all of the children have to be coaxed or induced to try anything they have not tasted before, some reject food altogether in the form of normal meals and for long periods will only eat such things as biscuits. We had one child who, according to her mother, previous to starting school had eaten only chocolate digestive biscuits and drunk only water for three years. It is usually easy to see why the parents have felt unable to tackle this problem; often it is because they are so relieved that the child is accepting any food from them that they prefer to go on supplying the biscuits or accept that he picks food off their plate rather than risk the child refusing to eat at all. Even those who do attempt to do something about it usually give up the effort because the child's resistance can usually outlast the parent's ability to tolerate withholding the favoured food. For the teacher it is easier to withhold the food and to insist on the child trying other kinds or to eat only from his own plate, since, to her, the child's acceptance or refusal of the food she offers does not have the same strong emotional significance as it has for his mother.

By means of a small 'shop' set up within the school the child's training in how to behave in a shop, and how to choose and pay for the things chosen is begun. We always use real money for this purpose and, although many of the packets of food, etc. are of necessity empty, the child is always rewarded at the end of the successful conclusion of a shopping exercise by being allowed to buy (and eat) real biscuits, sweets, fruit or such things as potato crisps. Even the smallest children begin this training early in their school life. All this is preparatory to taking the children into the town to shop, or to go into a café or restaurant. The teacher is again better able to tolerate or

105

deal with critical public comment if things go wrong (as they will initially) than is the mother. This training is very important because it is a great relief to the whole family when they can, eventually, take the child with them into the town, knowing that problems are unlikely to arise.

We also, whenever it is possible, try to use public transport for some of our outings. Many of the children prove to have never been on a train or a bus and therefore have absolutely no idea of all the activities that this involves, such as finding the right stop, recognising the bus you need, crossing the road safely, paying fares, etc. Incidentally, it is important to check that you are, in fact, teaching the thing that you assume you are teaching. I well remember my own stupidity when I confidently thought that I was teaching the children to interpret and react to traffic light signals, when in fact I was doing no such thing, because the children were only responding to my instructions! It was only when I kept still and, in reply to the children's question, told them that I was waiting for them to tell me when it was safe to cross and why, that their real training began.

The use of conditioning techniques

The term 'conditioning techniques' used in the most general sense, refers to a rag-bag of approaches to the study of human behaviour and of methods of attempting to direct it for purposes of therapy or education, etc. A variety of theoretical models are involved, not by any means entirely consistent with one another (or at least not obviously so). It is not, therefore, surprising that several different methods of using 'conditioning' techniques in order to modify human behaviour have been developed, and that each of them seems to have a certain value if used in an appropriate context for an appropriate purpose. The central notion common to all the conditioning approaches is that forms of behaviour which can be 'rewarded' tend to increase in frequency. However most schools of behaviouristic psychology tend to be highly suspicious of a term such as 'reward' which implies that the experience associated with the stimulus influences behaviour. The term 'reinforcement' is usually preferred in the sense that if behaviour 'A' tends to increase in frequency if it is often followed by stimulus 'X' then 'X' is said to be acting as a reinforcer for 'A'. This is an important distinction because it draws attention to the fact that 'X' need not be experienced as pleasurable; there is evidence that behaviours can be reinforced by stimuli of which the subject seems to be quite unaware.

The term 'reward' being suspect, it is not altogether consistent that some conditioning techniques are based on the notion of aversive (unpleasant) stimuli. It is held that the frequency of an undesired behaviour can be reduced if it is associated with an aversive stimulus, for example by making unpleasant stimulation a consequence of the undesired behaviour. This is one of the techniques frequently used by so-called 'behaviour therapists'. Those who stress the 'operant' approach to conditioning theory on the other hand, make no use of the notion that behaviour can thus be 'stamped out' by using aversion stimuli. They do, however, believe that the cessation of an aversion stimulus acts as a reinforcer — for example, a rat may be conditioned to press a particular lever, not only if he is frequently reinforced by obtaining food when he does so, but also if pressing the lever switches off a mild electric shock or other unpleasant stimulus. This particular kind of reinforcement which arises when a stimulus is removed rather than when it is given is known as 'negative reinforcement'.

The following are some examples of the use of conditioning methods for altering the behaviour of autistic children. Lovaas and his colleagues demonstrated in their set of well-known experiments how aversion techniques could be used to reduce self-destructive behaviours. In these experiments mild electric shocks were applied to the children's feet as soon as they began self-mutilation and were only switched off when they stopped. Later the experimenter called out 'No' at the same time as the shock was administered, in this way associating the verbal command with the aversive stimulus. Eventually the use of shocks could be discontinued as the secondary control was then all that was needed to obtain the desired effect. This is an extreme example of the technique which can only be properly applied in a clinic or treatment situation and which is of value for severely afflicted children who have not responded to other forms of control. Less severe forms of the technique can be used with success in the classroom and the home.

An application of negative reinforcement used to modify the behaviour of a child who was not behaving in a way required of him would be the application of an aversive stimulus (such as a form of restraint) which is only removed when the desired behaviour is emitted. Alternatively the same result could be achieved by the reinforcement of all desired behaviours. This is frequently used in the attempts to develop speech in autistic children. Initially any attempt to reproduce a sound is immediately reinforced; later this only happens when the sound or word is accurately produced. Many things can be used as reinforcers other than sweets or biscuits, etc.; for example, we have at present a small boy for whom the most effective reinforcer is an old envelope which he can tear up!

However, because of the difficulties of applying behaviouristic models consistently to the subtleties of the behaviour of autistic children, it is often easier to discuss them in terms of cognitive learning theory models and this is the form that will be used for the rest of this discussion. In the special context of autism it is worth noting that rewards that are usually effective with 'normal' children (such as sweets, food or the praise or approval of the person dealing with the child) may not serve. Most conditioning theorists would regret the use of concepts such as attention, motivation and the like in connection with attempts to explain such atypical reactions. However, for the psychologist or teacher who is not a disciple of any of the conditioning schools while yet interested in the methods involved, the use of the terminology of cognitive psychology may be permitted. To all appearances if these techniques are to be successful and to lead on to generalisation it is as if the most important thing is that the child must want the reward that you are using and for this purpose many things will serve. On admission to the school, we have found many of the children are so withdrawn that nothing has any meaning for them as a reward. We, therefore, do not attempt to use conditioning techniques until such time as the child is responsive to the teacher and sufficiently motivated and interested to make it possible to offer him meaningful rewards. With the autistic children we have frequently found that, at a later stage, the child is feigning indifference to an offered and previously 'wanted' reward rather than comply with the teacher's requests. When that stage comes we find that the child is attempting to use a controlling mechanism and we therefore refuse to accept this assumed lack of interest and insist on his staying in the situation until he has done what is required and accepted the reward. It is important to be sure who is controlling whom! I well remember in my earlier days of working with these children falling into this particular trap. I would spend a long time with a previously mute child working with her and encouraging her to talk so that I could reward her, until I suddenly realised that it was operating quite the other way around and she was, in fact, rewarding me, for giving her my exclusive attention, by finally giving me what I wanted. From then on I strictly limited the time which I gave to her in this way, warning her throughout that this limit was being approached and, when it was reached, withdrawing immediately and completely refusing to start again until I had decided it was time to do so. It took quite a while for her to accept this change but her progress in every way speeded up once she did. I had learnt a useful lesson also! We regard operant conditioning techniques as one of several equally valuable means of teaching autistic children, provided they are used at the most appropriate stage of the child's recovery and with a child who responds to this technique. In a sense we have found that they are most valuable as a means of speeding up progress with a child who is in fact apparently moving away from the critical features of autism. They might also be the only way of eliminating or eliciting a certain area of behaviour, as Lovaas appears to demonstrate.

PART 2

Communication—The development of speech and language

So far in this chapter I have discussed the methods we use to attempt to develop relationships and to initiate responsive behaviour. When working with autistic children the other essential task is to attempt to develop speech and language or, if

109

this proves to be impossible, some form of communication. The severely withdrawn autistic child not only does not communicate either verbally or with non-verbal signals, he also appears to be completely lacking in any wish to do so. His only 'contact' with other people (if indeed it can be called such) is to use them in an inhuman way, as a tool or an extension of his own arm, for example, to supply them with the things they cannot mechanically get for themselves. When we first start working with such a child we submit to this manipulation, but we never stop verbalising what we are doing as we do it. This seems to me to be vitally important for at least two reasons. First, because in this way the child is being given constant verbal stimulus—this is particularly necessary since in many cases the fact that the child has shown no sign of attending in any way to speech has often resulted in all attempts at verbal communication being abandoned. Second, the speech that is offered in this way has an immediate and practical relevance directly linked to something which the child wants and is attending to. At this stage communication is at best a one-way process. At times one even doubts this, since it is a long time before the child gives any sign of listening to what is being said. Constant verbalising is carried on during every activity throughout the day, and as the child begins to form relationships and become responsive, so he tends to give more cues that he is listening. At this point we start to encourage the child to try to say something. For example, if the child has manipulated you to reach a cup for him, as you do it you are saying, 'Oh, so you want a cup—here is the cup', then if he is looking at you or obviously listening it is important to continue as you hold it out to him with, 'Come on, now you say cup.' Any attempt to say it, no matter how rudimentary is immediately rewarded.

From then on the child is encouraged to try to ask for everything, and although initially any sound is accepted, as the child becomes more willing to try so the teacher can begin to correct his efforts and withhold both the reward and the things he wants until a more accurate attempt is made. It is normally at this point when the child has become co-operative that in our school the speech therapist begins to take him for individual sessions. From then on she and the teacher are working together, each supplementing what the other is doing. The most difficult part is to induce the child to make the first responsive sound. We have found that a child who does not respond to encouragement to repeat what you have said, will sometimes do it if you deliberately give an incorrect response to his manipulation. To return to the example, if instead of taking down the cup you pick up the thing next to it instead, the child will become angry, and if you then say, 'Well why didn't you say it was the cup you wanted', they will often do just that. We have found frequently that if the child is angry enough or frightened enough they will speak. One of my staff put it in this way, 'When they really need the words they use them.' It seems that a strong emotional reaction frees the child from his inhibitions and makes it possible for him to talk. We have often wished that the same effect could be produced in some other way (perhaps by the use of adrenalin?) since it is obviously both impossible and undesirable to keep the child in a constant state of fear or anger in order to keep him talking, even assuming it would have a continuous effect.

The use of music in developing speech

We use music in many ways in our attempt to develop verbalisation. Most autistic children do seem to respond spontaneously to music; many of the parents report that they have found it to be the only thing that will calm the children or hold their attention apart from their own obsessional behaviours. We have found the same thing. Although at first the children just listen and rock to the music after a while they will join hands with the teacher and the solitary rocking becomes a simple rhythmical response. Clapping to the music follows from this and then easy singing games, one-to-one at first, then in a small group. We introduce percussion instruments as soon as possible—this helps not only to establish rhythm but also gives practice in sequencing and repeating sound patterns, an essential skill to establish if speech is to develop. Several children have begun to sing the words of songs before they have begun to talk. We have also found that the children often first respond to sung verbal instructions, rather than spoken ones. The likelihood of this happening is very much increased if you sing them to a tune which the child has shown that he likes. Many of the children seem to hum quietly a tune of their own composition, and if this is the case and you sing all that you wish to say to the child to his own tune, it is possible to obtain an immediate and sustained response. In addition to the value it has in helping to develop speech the use of music has other benefits. It helps to increase imitative and responsive behaviour, provides an opportunity for the child and the teacher to do together something that the child enjoys, frequently helps the child to develop a freer and more relaxed movement other than his original rigid rocking, and is often the first activity involving other children that the child joins in willingly.

Gestures and speech development

Unlike deaf children or aphasic children who tend to use mime, signs or gestures, spontaneously developed as alternate means of communication, autistic children never do. It seems to me that this is the result of their lack of any desire, or perhaps, unfelt need to communicate rather than any lack of ability to develop these alternate forms. Communication only takes place within relationships; if therefore one of the main symptoms of your handicap is an impaired ability to form relationships you are not likely to feel any need to communicate. However, even when autistic children are beginning to relate and to act responsively they still do not appear to resort to signs, but rather persist in trying to pull you over to show you directly what it is they require from you. In order to encourage children to learn how to place new sounds correctly in their mouth and to control the expulsion of their breath in making sounds, they are sometimes taught gestures to aid the process, such as blowing across their hand or placing their finger on their lip in a particular way. We have found that these techniques tend to confuse rather than help autistic children, since they seem to be unable to decide what it is that you wish them to do, and get extremely agitated when they continue to repeat the correct gesture but without the sound (which was the object of the exercise) and are clearly not giving you what you want. They also seem to be completely literally minded and far more willing to repeat things that have an obvious practical value for themselves than to continue to practise sounds which would have the ultimate effect of improving their articulation.

Audiology

The fact that so many of these children neither speak nor respond normally to sound stimuli means that the possibility of a hearing loss must always be kept in mind. It is not easy to test their hearing, since they are often very frightened by the presence of the audiologist and the sight of the earphones. All their characteristic resistance to anything new comes to the fore. We therefore have arranged that the audiologist visits and sees every child at six-monthly intervals. If the child shows the slightest reluctance we do not attempt to get him to wear the earphones but use the audiometer rather like a musical instrument and let the child hear the range of sounds, at the same time making quite sure that he realises that the audio-meter is the source of the sound. This usually calms and interests the child and allows us to make a very rough judg-ment as to whether they can hear or not. It is at this time that we look for the pupillar reflex reaction if the child gives no obvious response. Most of the children seem to have unusually good long-term memory and so recognise the audiologist and his equipment on the second visit; by the third visit they will usually accept the earphones. The problems are not all over yet, however, for on the whole they are still unable either to say when they hear the sound, or to respond to the instruction to take a bead from a rod or move a toy car, as they hear it. The same confusion arises as to which instruction you wish them to follow that has already been described. We have found that if you give them no instruction but simply start the investigation, they will produce their own response. Some, for example, turn their head or their eyes in the direction of the stimulus, others may hum the note as they hear it. We feel that if we have consistent results on three consecutive audiograms then we have a true assessment of the child's hearing. We have also found as an interesting by-product that you can get an objective measure of the effects of a traumatic incident on a

113

disturbed child since there is a significant change in their audiogram during periods of stress. Although we have found some children with loss on some frequencies on the whole the autistic children prove to have very acute hearing. With regard to their speech this is especially interesting since the observation is often made that the speech of an autistic child at the beginning sounds very like that of a deaf child in its lack of inflection and poor intonation. I would suggest that one possible alternate reason for this is the rigidity of their mouth and lack of flexibility in their tongue and lip movements. It is at odds with their ability to sing and needs active speech therapy to remedy it.

Echolalia and 'speech' which is not language

There are some autistic children who are not mute but who nevertheless do not use the speech they appear to have in order to communicate. These are the children whose speech mainly consists of 'echolalia' i.e., an exact recitation of something which they have heard. This can immediately follow the hearing or may be 'delayed' for any length of time. There is no limit to the number of times it can be repeated. At times the child merely seems to be acting as a recording/reproducing machine and quite unaware of the content of what he is repeating. We had one boy who would repeat in its entirety the whole of the news he had heard on television the night before; we have at the moment a little girl who will pick up a telephone and give what is probably an exact reproduction of a conversation she has overheard. In her case it appears to be uncannily accurate, since she changes the tone of her voice, pauses as if listening, laughs, exclaims, etc. If you heard her without seeing her you would be quite convinced that you had heard her mother holding a genuine phone conversation. Yet in neither of these cases did the child have any comprehension of what he and she were saying. This form of echolalia has nothing to do with expressive language. The child appears to hear, store and then reproduce quite inappropriately something that has apparently no meaning for him. It also has no practical use in the attempt to develop verbal communication, apart from showing you that there is no impairment of the

114

child's hearing or ability to talk. There is, however, another form of echolalia which can be used for in this instance the child's echolalic statement is in fact a communication. An example of this is the often quoted habit these children have of repeating a question instead of making a statement, 'Do you want a biscuit?' for example, meaning 'I want a biscuit.' It is relatively easy to teach a child who has achieved this much to use the correct form, for the words have a genuine meaning and there is a motivated attempt to make a verbal communication. There are instances when it is necessary to take positive action against the use of echolalia, and these are the times when the child is using it as an avoiding or manipulating mechanism, or as a barrier between the teacher and the thing she wishes him to do or say. Experience and knowledge of the child enables the teacher to recognise that this is the case and it is necessary then to refuse to accept this evasion and to insist on the child's compliance. At times this is more easily achieved if, once you have seen that the child is now willing to respond, you 'cue' him in some way to initiate the response.

The use of conditioning techniques in speech development

In this section on speech development the point has already been made that all speech used with the child is directly related to what is happening. Films have been shown on television where this does not seem to be the case, and where the child is being asked to say a particular word decided upon by the therapist. In fairness it should be said that in these films the child eventually does. There is, however, no indication that the child was in any way interested in the object he was required to name. There is quite a lot of evidence that there is no generalisation of words acquired in this way and that it is possible for a child to have a vocabulary of twenty or more single words, but no expressive language for these words are only spoken in response to the stimulus by means of which they were learnt. We had a classic example of this in our school when we admitted a child who had learnt several words in a stimulus/response way. One of these was the word 'apple' and this particular girl loved apples. She did not, however, ever associate the word apple with a real apple although she invari-

115

ably responded with it every time she was shown the picture of an apple that had been used to teach her the word. On the other hand the same girl quite spontaneously said one day as she pushed my hand down towards her shoes, 'Do my laces up-a please-a.' This was an example of faulty speech, but correct use of language, whereas it seemed to me that the naming of the pictured apple was not speech at all but a learned reflex. This may have been a fault of the therapist, but the finding that generalisation does not take place is made too frequently for this to be a sufficient justification for a great deal of time and effort to be spent on using techniques which have such a limited end result, at the time when you are first trying to get an autistic child both to appreciate the point and purpose of speech, and motivated to attempt to learn it. We do, however, believe that operant conditioning techniques, both specifically applied in the speech therapy sessions and more generally but consistently throughout the day, both in school, and at home are invaluable in both inducing the child to use the speech he has acquired, and also in speeding up its development.

Alternative forms of language

Simple forms of sign language have long been used as a means of communication for those such as the deaf who have failed to develop speech. Some of them are now quite complex involving the use of grammatical constructions and such a wide vocabulary that it is possible to express abstract ideas as well as make purely practical statements. One such, now becoming more widely used, is the Paget-Gorman system. Since with every effort being made to teach speech to mute autistic children there are some who do not learn to talk, such alternative systems should be considered. There is the general argument that no matter how flexible such a system may be, it will always have a very limited application since it can only be used with other people who have learned the system and, outside the school and possibly the home, such people will be very few. When using the Paget-Gorman system it is stressed that the appropriate verbal communication must be used simultaneously. In this way it is hoped that the development of what may prove to be a more easily acquired form of communication will lead on to the development of speech. Some success has been reported with ESN (S) and aphasic children. There appears to be two possible reasons why it may not be as successful with autistic children. One is their negativism which puts great obstacles in the way of the successful use of any technique which involves imitative behaviour, the other is the difficulty already discussed of getting autistic children to link two activities meaningfully. We have tried it in a limited way with selected children who were willing to copy, but to date we have not found that it has had any great success. The children have learnt to make some of the symbols correctly but they have not used them spontaneously to communicate. One reason may well be that they are not having enough stimulus to do so, for it is not possible in our set-up for everyone they come in contact with throughout the day to communicate with them by means of the system. It would be most interesting and useful to know what results are achieved if the technique can be more consistently and rigidly applied than we have found practically possible.

Further development

Once the child is responsive, relating, interested in various activities, and developing verbal comprehension, with — hopefully — some expressive language — more formal teaching can be started. At this stage many factors will need to be considered in deciding what are the best methods to be used with each individual child, one of the most important being the child's intellectual potential. We try to develop an individual programme geared to each child's needs. For example, we attempt to decide whether to use a visual or a phonic approach to reading, or a combination of both. These, however, are the kinds of decision which all teachers are commonly making so they will not be discussed at any length here. In many ways the child can now be regarded as any other child at this stage would be. Certain autistic features will still be present, however, and they can either operate positively or be an obstacle in the way of achievement. One such could be the child's obsessive desire to persist with an activity which interests him. This must be monitored and if necessary controlled. We had one

117

boy who quite correctly decided that his limited vocabulary was holding him back in every other subject. After some discussion the boy accepted a reasonable target and set out to learn a hundred new words a week. His initial wish was to learn at least twice that number. This he could only have achieved with difficulty at the expense of everything else. In accepting and achieving a possible target he used constructively and to his own great advantage one of the characteristics of his earlier autistic behaviour. The same tendency can be seen at an earlier educational stage when the child can be most unwilling to leave one activity and move on to another. Similarly, he finds it very difficult to see why he must 'take turns' or share with other children the very things that the teacher has, with great care and difficulty, encouraged him to enjoy. This is one of the particular problems which calls for fine judgment (which will come with experience) on the part of teachers working with autistic children. There is a danger that when you have managed to achieve anything, you are so pleased that both you and the child will stand still at that point, and this has to be resisted. The child will normally see no need at all to 'move on'. The teacher therefore must see that he does, for unless and until the child can learn to be more adaptable and flexible, and prepared to share, he will have great difficulty in taking his place in normal situations. In the earlier stages of our teaching programme we do tend to keep to a regular structure and order of activities. Later this programme is deliberately made more flexible, so, although on each day the child is, in fact, carrying out a very similar range of activities the order in which they are done is constantly varied. At first this leads to many protests and attempts on the part of the child to insist on keeping to the established pattern. In time though the change is accepted and the child is able to work happily no matter in what order the day is planned. It does tend to be more difficult to get him to appreciate the need to share, and some of the children show great ingenuity in hiding the things they want to monopolise. One child had us all totally baffled until we 'caught' her one day unscrewing the head of a large doll, in whose body she had carefully hidden the things she did not want to share! Persistent encouragement over a long period of time with much praise whenever the child complies seems to be the answer but it does take a very long time, and even when the child has learnt to share he often makes it clear that he does not really see why he should!

Another problem can be the children's tendency to interpret everything that is said to them with complete literalness. They have had no experience of verbal humour, or exaggeration, or of learning to accept implied generalisations. For example, most children told to, 'Eat up — get on with your potatoes' will understand the instruction to apply to the whole meal; an autistic child might well just eat the potatoes and wait for the next instruction. An exasperated but playful, 'Drop dead!' from another child can cause real horror and confusion. In one case I knew, great problems in understanding arose between a mother and her autistic child when, the child coming home one day and being unable to see the baby, took literally the threat she had overheard her over-stressed mother to utter and asked if this was the day she had killed the baby because it would not stop crying. This tendency to complete literalness tends to persist and must always be borne in mind by anyone talking to the children even after many of their autistic mannerisms appear to have gone. However it also seems to give them an unusual integrity since it ensures that their verbal statements and responses are also literally accurate. I remember one girl who was longing for a particular cake, refusing it, since she was only offered it on condition that she made a certain promise, and could not do so because as she said, 'I might not keep it.' She was shocked and confused when told she could have the cake for being honest. The nuances of the situation were so outside her experience that they were beyond her comprehension. However, as time went on she came much nearer to understanding and accepting this sort of incident (which would have been quite commonplace to any child growing up in the normal way) particularly perhaps as the adults working with her had become more aware of her needs in this respect, and were making conscious efforts to deal with them.

Conclusion

It would be wrong and misleading to appear to be suggesting

119

that some autistic children taught in the ways suggested above become normal in the sense that they act in every way as an average child would, putting on one side all discussion as to whether any child ever does. All of those whom I have known personally, even those who appear to be most successful, tend to be over-anxious and insecure, and to find it difficult to associate on equal terms in any social group. This is partly due to their anxiety but also to a large extent to lack of this kind of experience during their growing years. In spite of this problem they can live independently in the community and are capable of earning their own living. Given support they also enjoy some forms of social activity. Most importantly perhaps, they want to be part of the community and are looking forward in the normal way to marriage, although not so frequently to parenthood.

There are others who do not achieve this but can either live as contributing members in a sheltered form of community life, of the kind provided in the Steiner or CARE villages, or will continue to benefit and progress in an environment such as that described by Sybil Elgar in the next chapter. A few appear to make no useful progress at all and when their families can no longer contain them they have to be found a long-term hostel or hospital placement. Some of the possible reasons why there is this variation of outcome are discussed in other chapters of this book. Perhaps as our knowledge and skill grows it will be reduced. The important thing is that the opportunity for the attempt to be made should be available for every child who needs it.

References

1   Jeanne Simmons, Statement, 'To see where they are going', Director, Linwood Children's Center, Ellicot City, Maryland, USA.
2   C. R. Ferster, 'Positive reinforcement and behavioural deficits of autistic children', *Child Development*, 1961, 32, pp. 437–56.

6 Further education and training for the autistic adolescent

SYBIL ELGAR

For the normal child the classroom is a training period for life but (the development of autistic children is retarded on all levels and, for the majority, their special classroom is only the beginning of learning how to learn and there is not enough time before the normal school leaving age to overcome the lag in maturation.) Facilities for the 'child' vary but generally when there is such provision, the approach is ongoing, positive and hopeful. However for the autistic school 'leaver', the situation changes and facilities are extremely limited. From 1965 to 1974 I was Headmistress of the National Society for Autistic Children's first school in London. During these years, ten of our pupils were transferred to normal school situations and continued to make progress but as time went on it became increasingly apparent that although the remaining pupils had made some progress according to ability and degree of handicap, they would not be ready to cope with the demands and pressures of life outside school when they reached the statutory leaving age.

Teenage years for the autistic adolescent are difficult ones and their inability to cope with the physical and psychological changes of this time retards the rate of educational and social progress during the later school years. At the time when their need for security and the continuation of a structured and systematic educational and social programme is greatest, authority decides it is time to leave school. Far too many are left at home with or without the provision of an Adult Training Centre or are admitted to sub-normality hospitals although they do not require full-time medical care. In these circumstances the need to plan and formulate continued educational facilities for the older child became a priority. A

121

small group of parents of the young people at the London school formed a working committee to find suitable premises for this purpose, and to decide on the best way to raise the necessary capital for the project.

After two or three years of searching, the right place was found and Somerset Court, the first residential centre catering exclusively for the needs of autistic adolescents, opened in August 1974.

Somerset Court is a pioneer establishment. Prior to its set-up there was no residential provision in this country for autistic adolescents and adults, except where they could be accepted with other handicapped people, and such organisations tend mainly to accept young people who are capable of higher performance levels as regards work, and a greater command of self-organisation, than is usually found in autistic persons. Adult Training Centres vary according to the number of trained staff and the amount of space available. It is true that some centres providing viable situations combining work, education and social programmes accept a few autistic adolescents, but they are in the minority and the need for such places is far greater than the available provision.

The abilities, social competence and degree of disturbance of the residents at Somerset Court cover a wide range; to deal with this we provide a comparatively high ratio of carefully selected staff together with the individual programmes to suit various needs.

Residential centre at Somerset Court

The Centre is in Brent Knoll, Somerset. It is not geographically isolated, being about two and a half miles from Burnham-on-Sea and about fifteen minutes drive away from Weston-super-Mare; the M5 motorway runs past the boundary of the cricket pitch. We have a large house with thirty-nine rooms in twenty-two acres of land, there is also a cottage as an annexe and stables and outbuildings.

The first floor of the main house is used for bedrooms, bathrooms, showers and toilets, television room and common room for senior residents and accommodation for house-care staff. The bedrooms are one-, two-, three- and four-bedded. In the cottage we have kitchen and bathroom facilities, a young people's common room, two bedrooms for residents (two-bedded) and accommodation for house-care staff.

On the ground floor of the main house we have three class-rooms, three workrooms, office accommodation, laundry, a staff and a residents' common room, a medical room, games, music and dancing hall, a kitchen, and dining and recreational hall.

Classrooms can be used, when necessary, as workshops, and a woodwork area is housed in one of the outbuildings. About six acres of land are now under cultivation to supply vegetables for our own consumption, and for sale in our garden centre; we have two portable greenhouses, two glasshouses and a fruit orchard. We have forty hens to provide eggs, budgerigars (rearing for sale), goats, guinea fowl and pheasants; we breed goldfish in the pond to sell and have thirty ducks of various kinds on the stream running through the grounds. We are about to start bee-keeping. In an existing outbuilding a garden centre has been started to produce and sell plants, shrubs, young trees, garden equipment, surplus produce and our own craft and cottage industries.

Residents

Residents begin the day at 7.30 a.m. from Monday to Friday, and 8.30 a.m. at the weekends. Breakfast is approximately one hour later and during this time they make beds, tidy the rooms, dust and hoover, wash and shave. Work starts at 9.30 a.m. with a mid-morning break from 10.30 to 11, lunch at 12.30 to 1.30 p.m., tea at 4 p.m. and the evening meal at 6.30 p.m., followed by, in due course, bedtime drinks and biscuits or cakes. Bedtimes vary according to age and sleep requirement and are from 9.30 p.m. to 10.30–11 p.m.

Parents can visit every third Sunday and there are optional long weekends every five weeks. There are also three or four short-stay periods each year at home or elsewhere away from the Centre. Letters are exchanged with home every week and where applicable there is telephone communication.

The residents have all been diagnosed by various authorities as autistic and some have additional handicaps. At present

123

they all come from the London area or the Home Counties and have been in my care for a number of years, some since they were 4 or 5. We prepared them for the move to Somerset Court well beforehand by constantly talking about the transfer, providing a model of the new house together with pictures of the grounds, and counting off the months, the weeks and the days. We arranged one or two visits to the site before the change, and the majority settled in quite happily and we experienced difficulty only with those of the young people whom we expected to react badly.

Our new community began with some advantages:

(i) the residents were used to structure and routine;

(ii) being aware of the potential and personalities of each one, we were able to continue immediately their individual educational and vocational instruction;

(iii) three of my previous staff moved with me and the children had known them for some years.

We would like to increase our numbers but with our present accommodation we have the full complement of young people allowed by the various authorities, i.e. twenty-three residents, eighteen young men and five young women whose ages range from 11 to 22 years. Fourteen of this number are over 16 and nine under. I find this spread of age is good as it provides stimulation for the staff in an on-going situation with the younger and more malleable child. It has advantages too from the residents' point of view since it provides a situation where the more exuberant youngsters can interact with and involve the older and more withdrawn residents.

At present our residents can be divided into the following groups as regards productive and social viability, but it is hoped that as teaching and training continues some of them will show improvement.

Group A   Those able to work in a given situation with a minimum of supervision, and able to contribute to a social situation and with a fair degree of independence.

Group B   Those who can contribute in some areas but who require varying degrees of support in work situations and/or help with self-care and social situations.

Group C   Those who are very limited — needing constant attention to complete simple routine tasks and lacking independence and social competence.

Group B and C include young people with marked behavioural difficulties, and all but one of Group C are over 16. Since the move one of the younger residents has been transferred to Group B as he has developed a much more positive attitude and is acquiring some new skills and a greater degree of independence; there is also an older girl, still included in Group C, who is beginning to contribute for limited periods to one or two of the work programmes, and whose behaviour pattern is a little more stable.

Additional handicaps

We have at Somerset Court two girls and one boy with epilepsy and one girl to whom something very odd seems to be happening. All of these four young people at the present time are included in the categories B and C.

Girl aged 22   Normal development until eight months, then developed petit mal. Her fits are reasonably controlled by drugs.

Boy aged 16   First generalised motor convulsion in January 1975 and was admitted to hospital. There they found bilateral spasticity in the legs and asymmetrical reflexes. The spasticity resolved over a few days. At present the fits are controlled by drugs.

Girl aged 16   First fit in 1967, controlled by drugs. This girl is very difficult prior to her periods, defecating, head banging and throwing herself to the ground and occasionally acting aggressively towards others.

Girl aged 16   Has periods of hyper-activity, becoming extremely agitated, with obsessional touching, followed by either weeping and/or aggression. Starts such attacks by looking very pale, twitching and perspiring. She is also worse at period times. At present she is receiving drug treatment.

125

We also have a deaf boy who in addition suffers from Retinitis Pigmentosa, and a 17-year-old boy who has additional disorders of congenital dislocation of the hip and cerebral palsy of the hypotonic type.

Staff

With such a mixed range of residents obviously a high staff ratio is required, and we have a well-balanced, practical yet supportive staff with different expertises. We utilise their abilities with our several programmes; and they are also asked to teach each other their skills so that the overall production is not interrupted by individual absences. For our twenty-three residents we have: one principal, two full-time teachers, five part-time teachers, one part-time occupational therapist, one gardener/handyman (contractor with own staff), secretary, book-keeper, cook and two weekend day relief staff, plus two senior house parents and three junior house staff.

It is not possible to be too specific regarding future staffing. Obviously as time goes on teachers will be less in demand and tradesmen and craft workers more appropriate, and it is hoped that more of the tasks at present undertaken by staff can be transferred to the residents; we have already replaced all cleaning and laundry staff by some of our young people, and one or two of our older boys are proving to be useful within the garden and grounds.

The full-time teaching staff are not residential and they work normal hours with ten weeks' holiday during the year allocated over four periods. All training staff, apart from the gardener, are part-time. House care staff are residential and work a thirty-five hour week.

New staff

When we first opened I was fortunate enough to be able to ensure continuity by providing a teacher or house-parent from my previous school and/or myself in every situation. My senior house staff (who moved with me) were able to give the necessary support and training to newly appointed junior care staff.

Apart from personal qualifications I consider the main

126

essentials required from teaching and training staff are optimism, determination and a realistic understanding of the residents' potential and limitations.

In addition to long discussions about individual residents, all new teaching staff are given a written account of each child's development on all levels, together with work sheets to provide individual patterns for extension. House care staff are informed of the degree of self-care and social competence that each resident has achieved, so that existing standards can be maintained and, whenever possible, extended.

Aims at the Centre

Our aims in dealing with these young people are:
   (i) to provide a comprehensive environment continuing educational, vocational, social and self-care instructions suited to individual needs;
  (ii) to provide a balanced programme of education, work and leisure;
 (iii) to make each one aware as far as possible of the importance of their own contribution to the community;
 (iv) to train the more competent to be fitted to integrate into society, to help the less able to lead fuller, happier and useful lives within the community and to protect and improve the quality of life for a minority unable to contribute on any level.

With such a heterogeneous group of residents, it will be obvious that some profit more from our situation and programmes than others.

The community is designed to meet the special needs of three main groups at different levels of competence and achievement. They are:

Group A   the least handicapped;
Group B   those who are less able in performance and more disturbed;
Group C   those with a considerable degree of disability and disturbance.

Most of the residents are within our Group B and it is they (with a few exceptions) who have made the most marked progress.

127

Some of the members of Group C do not appear at present to benefit from any form of education or training, but our environment is a personalised one and a more pleasant alternative than hospitalisation. At least within this setting they have not regressed.

Training programmes

At present we have seven residents for whom the Department of Health and Social Security are responsible, the others are still within the control of the Department of Education and Science.

Work and training programmes for all embrace as wide a field as possible, but we have only been in operation for just over a year so there has not yet been time to explore all the opportunities for creating work routines. We are beginning to find the right kind of balanced work/leisure programme for some of the older residents, and I give a specimen of a weekly work programme for two of our young people (p. 129).

Time is allowed for a structured educational programme designed to help the older residents to function more adequately in daily living. They need continuing instruction in language concepts, reading, writing, 'time', number and money. How long it will be necessary to continue such instruction is difficult to foresee, but as long as the person concerned is 'learning' then he surely should be taught. Growing older has not helped the autistic young people in this Centre to overcome their inability to generalise and much of the teaching needs to be mechanical and repetitive, followed by appropriate practical application.

(i) *Language*

Difficulty with the use and understanding of language persists into adolescence and adulthood. A new environment requires more and different words for personnel, places, occupations, tools and social occasions. The residents need time and training to understand unfamiliar speech patterns of new staff, and staff in turn need time to appreciate the limitations in the understanding of speech by individual residents.

128

Boy aged 20

	a.m.	lunch	p.m.	tea		recreation
Monday	prepare and discuss T/T for week. Needlework, running repairs, buttons, etc.		horse-riding/ stool seating			games
Tuesday	swimming A/S		woodwork and maintenance		CLEARING PROGRAMME	youth club
Wednesday	printing		garden and maintenance		CLEARING PROGRAMME	skittles
Thursday	music and craft		office work			television
Friday	garden and maintenance		cookery			
Saturday	A/S gardening		woodwork			games/dancing

(boiler maintenance every a.m. and p.m.)
A/S = academic subjects

Girl aged 17

	a.m.	lunch	p.m.	tea		recreation
Monday	laundry		ironing			games
Tuesday	swimming A/S		domestic work		CLEARING PROGRAMME	youth club
Wednesday	needlework		cookery		CLEARING PROGRAMME	skittles
Thursday	music/craft		domestic work			television
Friday	domestic work A/S		ironing			
Saturday	cookery		needlework			games/dancing

A/S = academic subjects

(ii) *Reading*

Autistic young people seldom read for pleasure but life will be more meaningful for them if they can read and understand directions, notices, newspapers and instructions and letters from home.

(iii) *Writing*

Residents need to write letters home and to write out their own timetables. Work is needed with the formation, size and spacing of letters, as well as with the construction of sentences. We aim to establish the relationship between talking, reading and writing.

(iv) *Money*

Shopping, fares on buses, pocket money, saving, buying clothes, and where appropriate the significance of wages, banks, etc.

(v) *Time*

Understanding the passage of time—daily routines, changing clothes, visiting days, weekends at home, weekend activities.

In addition to the educational curriculum, work programmes at present include:

1 *Domestic work*

Making up and changing beds, cleaning, setting and clearing tables, washing up, cookery and laundry. We use a production line method involving as wide a range of residents as possible, e.g. for cookery, some wash vegetables, chop, cut, mix and prepare, and the more able use the stove. We make our own marmalade, pickles and chutney, cakes and tarts. Laundry activity involves the collection of dirty linen, sorting, setting machines, using rotary and hand irons and folding and delivering. These programmes, if broken down and suitably allocated, are within the range of those even with low ability.

2 *Craft work*

Needlework, canework, weaving, stool seating, making jewellery, soft toys, suede and knitted items. We expected (and were proved right) that activities requiring repetitive mathematical patterns, such as some weaving and knitting, stool seating, cross stitching on canvas, would be within the ability range of the majority. All our goods are saleable and we are able to fulfil most orders.

3 *Animal husbandry*

Feeding and care of livestock.

130

4 *Gardening and garden centre*

Mowing (hand and driven motors), weeding, rotavating, planting, digging, collecting grass, bedding and potting plants, pulling vegetables, collecting fruit, etc. Animal husbandry and gardening work schedules are planned within the available facilities of the house and grounds.

6 and 7 *Woodwork and maintenance*

At present woodwork is on a simple level, and residents make seed boxes, bird houses and flower pot stands, key racks, etc. They mend furniture and equipment, paint fences and wood surfaces and varnish stool frames. As more funds become available we hope to extend this programme.

8 *Office work*

Typing and duplicating, stapling, sorting and folding.

9 *Printing*

Setting up of print and operating presses for stationery, tickets, notepaper, etc.

As time goes on we plan to extend some programmes and introduce others. Some routines have already been discontin-

Table 6.1   Residents participating in programmes

	Programme	Contributing residents
1	Domestic	16
2	Craft	15
3	Animal husbandry	1
4	Gardening	4
5	Using mower and rotavator	1
6	Woodwork and ⎱	6
7	Maintenance ⎰	
8	Office work and duplicating	5
9	Printing	3

ued because they were uneconomic. Several of our young people can contribute to three or four programmes, and we are finding out individual strengths and weaknesses.

As with the younger autistic child, nothing happens unless an adult makes it happen, and the adolescent needs to be taught every new skill and how to work. Some continue to resist attempting anything new and I have found the best way to overcome their lack of dependability and drive is to provide a teaching situation comprising order, consistency, manipulation, repetition and determination.

Behaviour problems

Some aspects of the autistic child's difficult behaviour tend to adjust as they grow older, such as eating and sleeping problems, but if others such as hyper-activity, aggression, destructiveness, temper tantrums, negativism, ritualistic and obsessional behaviour continue through to adolescence and adulthood, then these problems are much more difficult to control than with the younger child, and interfere with teaching and social programmes. Staff are left with a feeling of inadequacy whilst trying to cope with outbursts of aggression and are not likely to be encouraged to persist with teaching a large 18-year-old boy or girl, say, to dress or bath, if every attempt to do so is met by him/her hitting out, pulling hair, biting, kicking and scratching. Nor does it always help to have a number of staff, anxious to assist, converge upon the young person concerned, as this often prolongs and worsens the situation.

When a hyper-active young person rushes around, jumping up, hitting electric light fittings, grabbing fire extinguishers, equipment and curtains, it causes more damage than similar behaviour in a smaller child and it is not as easy to control. Explosive outbursts of screaming or roaring are more difficult to combat in an adolescent. It is a comparatively simple matter to pick up a screaming youngster and remove him to other surroundings, but impossible to take the same action with his larger counterpart. It is also a problem to find ways to stop some of our young people from tearing their clothes or bed linen during the night or in less supervised situations. Biting and breaking furniture and equipment can be checked with 1:1 staff ratio, but it is a staff-consuming exercise. Negativism too presents problems — a young child can be manipulated to go somewhere or to do something — not, so the adolescent.

With the young autistic child some obsessional and ritualistic behaviour can be used to his advantage, but the adolescent is controlled by his obsession to the exclusion of all else. Self-mutilation such as head banging, biting hands and arms, throwing themselves on to the floor, persist with some, and it is little consolation when dealing with these to remember that you have read somewhere, or that someone told you, to leave the head banger alone because he never hurts himself, when she/he has just broken a window or damaged a door with her/his head.

Obviously as the child grows he gets bigger and stronger, and difficulties in management increase. It has not been my experience that the behavioural problems of the adolescent can be managed as easily as those of the younger autistic child. We do find ways to control most of the time, but there is no handbook of rules for the management of behaviour — techniques are usually established by trial and error, and action that works on one occasion may worsen a situation in another. Autistic adolescents are emotionally unstable and immature but continuous rigid control will not help them to develop individuality and self-responsibility. As with normal adolescents, whenever possible it is better to avoid direct confrontation, to minimise the opportunities for rebellion, and to be alert to danger signals. However, behaviour breakdowns that interfere with the general running of the Centre and the interests of others cannot be accepted and the longer such behaviour continues the more it is reinforced and the overall stability and standards for all are adversely affected. I have found that the best way to terminate such a situation is to restrain and remove the young person concerned from his audience or alternatively, if this is physically impossible, remove the audience from him.

So far we have been able to handle any sex problems. Interest in sex is on an immature level and, as these young people are without guile, any unacceptable behaviour is easily observed, e.g. public exploration of other residents' bodies,

133

masturbation and so on. This behaviour is discouraged in as matter of fact a way as possible, and in the same way as they are asked to do, or not to do, anything else. The boys and young men in the main seem able to cope, but three out of five of the girls become very disturbed and frustrated prior to periods.

Social competence and training

The majority of our young people have through the years acquired some self-care competence and are maintaining and extending these skills, but further training is required with the right kind of response to social situation, e.g. the right kind of behaviour at dances, socials, theatres, in public transport, and other people's homes, the right kind of clothes to wear to suit the weather and occasion.

Self-care with our residents ranges from the capable to the dependent. We have thirteen residents who can make and change their beds without help, and who can wash, bath, and clean their teeth and shoes. Five need some help, two need support all the time and three need to have these services performed for them; the same three also need help to dress.

Apart from two residents, who know when and how to wash and dry their hair, this activity needs similar varying degrees of supervision. Two young men can shave themselves and two others need to be shaved. All the residents can take themselves to the toilet when necessary, although some need reminding of the necessary arrangements for personal hygiene and we still have some residents who wet and foul their beds.

They all use knives and forks and spoons for eating, but five need help with cutting food, spreading butter, etc.

Recreational activities

Most of our young people are not able to organise their leisure time activities. Within the community we arrange programmes involving TV, music, dancing, games, swimming, horse-riding and various outings and some time is allowed for all to do, or not do, as they wish. Eleven of our residents attend youth clubs and some of the older residents go to the local pub to play skittles once a week. I am not sure how much our young people profit from association with their normal contemporaries, but I feel it is a worthwhile exercise as the club members do work at involving our residents and enjoy doing so. We have a younger boy who goes to Cubs and attends the local school two afternoons a week, but he is more socially responsive than most of our older residents.

We have been fortunate in settling at our present location because of the sustained interest and goodwill of those living in the vicinity. Individual youngsters are invited to homes and to join in family outings, groups are invited to local functions and we are included in all that goes on in the neighbourhood. We, in turn, invite our friends back to the Centre. We are able to take most of our young people out and about—some obviously enjoy these occasions, others just accept them. We have a few who do not enjoy the kind of entertainment offered or the involvement of other people and I believe little would be gained by insisting on their inclusion. Instead we arrange separate smaller group outings for them such as rides in the minibus, walking, swimming or record sessions.

Location of a community

The choice of an urban or rural setting for a community is a matter of opinion and availability—obviously there is need for both, but I have found that a rural area such as ours has some advantages, e.g. the local general practitioner both is, and has time to be, personally interested and concerned and visits the school frequently so that the children get used to seeing him around. To avoid long waits in the surgery he either comes to the Centre to give advice on a personal visit or gives it on the telephone, and if he is in any doubt he arranges for specialists to call. Other supporting services are involved and give help and advice, such as for example the consultant psychiatrist for the Somerset area, the educational psychologist, representatives of the Department of Education, the Social Services Department and the Fire Officer. I have already mentioned how we are accepted by the local people, and fund raising and other assistance by the various organisations and by individuals is continuous.

Disadvantages

The nearest industrial centre is about nine miles away and there are no public bus routes which we could use to get there. At present this is not a problem as we have nobody in the centre who is ready to go to this kind of work.

We are about half a mile away from the bus route to the nearest town, but fortunately we have our own minibus. Apart from the village shops the nearest shopping centre is in Burnham, two and a half miles away.

Conclusions

Most autistic young people have continuing learning and social problems and here at Somerset Court a few of them have the opportunity to go on with all aspects of their education. The evidence so far indicates that seventeen of our young people have definitely profited from this further provision, although of course the degree varies according to the individual.

Recently we were able to obtain outside residential employment for one 18-year-old girl, and she now works as a domestic assistant in a private nursing home; a year ago this would not have been possible for her. So far she is doing well, and she is near enough to the Centre to be able to spend her free time with us. This is fortunate as she is still very vulnerable and needs a good deal of support and guidance in social situations. This outcome will not happen for all our residents but it is possible that one or two of the others may eventually require only residential and social support and be able to undertake selected work outside.

Some of the less capable residents have settled well and are slowly but surely developing social competence, and independence and acquiring new skills. They are able to work with less supervision and even though they cannot put a name to it they are beginning to appreciate the importance of the 'give and take' balance required in community living and their own part in the Centre.

On the other side of the coin six of our residents cannot at the present time contribute to the viability of the Centre in any

136

way and five of them are periodically disruptive, requiring a high ratio of skilled staff to control, protect and care for them. At this stage of their development teachers and tradesmen do not appear to be the right people to help them but neither do they require constant medical care. I wonder if the provision of a basic training unit within the Centre with different staff and programmes might help to adjust the overall balance and provide a more viable situation.

Such a unit would provide care while at the same time aiming to maintain existing individual social competence and skills; the degree of their ability to cope with simple work/social routines would help us to assess the readiness of individuals for assimilation back into the main stream as hopefully there is always the possibility of improvement at any age. If this provision could be made, the parents of the less able would be assured of the permanence and safety of the placement, the youngsters themselves relieved of pressure to conform to situations to which they are not suited. The specialised staff would have more time to get on with the job of teaching and training those able to benefit. If the community is to be a viable unit then future admissions must be selected from the more able and socially responsive young people. The alternative of taking more of the severely disturbed and retarded would change the character of the centre and the future outlook and opportunity for all would deteriorate.

Somerset Court is a pioneer venture and during this first year the situation has developed satisfactorily. Most of the residents are making overall progress and each day provides an opportunity for all to develop self-care skills, social adequacy, education and work training. The Centre is a happy one with an atmosphere of belonging and purposefulness but it can only cater for a few. Far too many autistic people are left without follow-up provision. More day and residential centres both in urban and rural areas are urgently needed to provide a comprehensive programme of further education and training. Failing this the time, effort and money allowed for suitable school provision is of little avail.

Case histories of three residents

Boy aged 18

This boy has been in my care since he was 5. At that time, he was very disturbed, hyper-active, destructive, without speech and completely unco-operative, and it was very difficult to take him out because of his unacceptable behaviour. Through the years he has made some progress, but at 18 his development remains immature. He can read and write, tell the time, knows days of the week, recognises coins and can work out shopping bills, but he does not understand the concept of the value of money or its use as a medium of exchange. At present he is included in parts of the gardening programme, all of the domestic programme, and he can weave oven gloves, make bathroom rugs and cross stitch bags. He uses speech mainly to ask for what he wants or to answer a question, but occasionally he makes a spontaneous observation.

His behaviour pattern has changed and he is inert rather than active. His performance on all levels is slow, but he does contribute to the Centre.

Social training. He is able to do most things for himself, albeit slowly and precisely, but he needs help with hair-washing. He enjoys swimming, cycling, music and dancing, accepts without enthusiasm social occasions such as the youth club and skittle evenings, and always behaves well.

Boy aged 16

He has been in my care since he was 4. When he was admitted he was hyper-active, not toilet-trained, without speech, completely self-absorbed, unable to feed or do anything for himself.

He is no longer hyper-active, but it has not been possible to extend his academic and occupational skills.

He can use a knife and fork to feed himself, but cannot cut with a knife nor spread butter or sandwich fillings. He needs help with dressing, undressing, washing, bathing, care of hair and teeth.

He does use the toilet during the daytime but is incontinent at night. Just a few months ago this boy had his first generalised motor convulsion, followed months later by another less severe fit. He is now receiving drugs and is calmer and more relaxed.

Girl aged 17

She has been in my care since she was 8. Before that time she was excluded from two special schools, one for psychotic children and an ESN school, because of her difficult and unpredictable behaviour. She was hyper-active, destructive and aggressive towards other children and although echolalic she did not use language to communicate, but since the transfer to Somerset Court she has made a great deal of progress and is now a happy, contributing member of the community, able to take care of herself and to be included in the domestic and needlework programmes. Her academic achievements consist of reading, writing, comprehension and use of money and the ability to weigh and measure. In addition she now has some appreciation of the value of time—she can tell the time and knows the days of the week and the months of the year. Although her conversation is limited and obsessional in subject matter, she does use speech for communication, can answer questions adequately and comprehend and comply with reasonably complicated verbal instructions. She works well and shows some initiative, and is now selective of the things she wants to do—refusing some activities and outings but asking for others, including the things she likes i.e. swimming, dancing and singing and listening to records. She prefers adult company to that of the other residents, but attends a local youth club where her behaviour is always acceptable.

7 Research and the teaching of autistic children

JILL BOUCHER AND LES SCARTH

Introduction

As noted in chapter 2, there is still considerable controversy about the condition variously named 'early infantile autism', 'childhood autism', or 'Kanner's syndrome'. In any discussion of autism, therefore, it is necessary at the outset to make clear what definition of the term 'autism' is being used. If this is not done, statements may be taken to apply to one group of children when they were intended to apply to some other group. Moreover, in any discussion, such as the present one, of research findings, it is important that findings which are cited should, as far as possible, refer to groups of children all of whom have been diagnosed on the same criteria.

Fortunately for present purposes, there has over the last five or ten years emerged something of a consensus view among those who report research, as to how the term 'autism' should be defined (Rutter, 1968; DeMyer, 1971; Wing, 1976a and b).

According to this definition the following features of behaviour must be present if autism is to be diagnosed:

1 a profound and general failure to develop social relationships;

2 language retardation with impaired comprehension, echoing, and pronoun reversal (e.g. using 'you' instead of 'I')';

3 ritualistic or compulsive phenomena.

All these behavioural features should, on the definition used here, have been present from infancy—that is from before the age of about $2\frac{1}{2}$ years. This concept of autism is agnostic as to causes, and accepts the possibility that the syndrome may arise in a variety of ways and show a variety of concomitant, or

140

additional, disabilities co-existing with the criterial features of the syndrome listed above. Concomitant disabilities are accepted as differing widely in individual children, but frequently include mental retardation and signs of brain dysfunction.

The purpose of the present chapter is to present some of the research findings concerning the group of children diagnosed autistic as described above. It is hoped that some of these findings might prove of interest to teachers and others working in day-to-day situations with these children. A secondary purpose of the chapter is to encourage communication and co-operation between teachers and research workers in this field. There is every reason for teachers to participate in research projects specifically related to teaching. There is also a need for teachers to contribute to observations on the basis of which theories as to the exact nature and development of autism can be developed and tested. Conversely there should be much that research can offer to teachers; all research into autism is carried out with eventual application in mind, and researchers may feel their work is wasted if those who care for and teach the children show little interest in what they have found out and in the problems they are attempting to elucidate.

A few general points on the research literature are made below, before going on to summarise some of the presently available findings which might be of interest.

Research is mainly concerned with attempting to establish reliable information about autism. Research workers may present and discuss theories about autism, but in the present state of knowledge at least, the actual research findings are more important than the theories. Research is concerned, moreover, to make observations which are *generally true* of all autistic children, or possibly true of different sub-groups of autistic children. They are therefore less concerned than teachers must be with each child's individual differences. For this reason, also, individual cases are rarely studied by research workers, who usually look at groups of autistic children and try to find out what they have in common with each other, and in what way they differ from groups of subjects who are not autistic.

Research may sometimes seem to deal with minutiae, or

141

with questions with no immediately obvious application, or perhaps to be merely confirming the obvious. However, accurate and detailed description requires that behaviour is analysed minutely as well as being understood in its main outlines. Often, analysis of small details of behaviour is only useful, or applicable, when several details can be fitted together to form a comprehensible picture, like a mosaic. Moreover, confirmation of what may be readily observed is essential before going on to further investigation of aspects which may not, perhaps, be so readily apparent.

Teachers need, therefore, to some extent to be patient with research. They also need to evaluate research reports critically. Research findings are not sacrosanct. Researchers are dealing with real (sometimes very difficult) children, just as teachers are, even though the rather dry 'scientific' language of research reports may tend to conceal this fact. Moreover, researchers are usually well-meaning but fallible people, who may quite unwittingly bias their results, or come to wrong conclusions. There is, therefore, a good deal of room for error in research findings, and for this reason teachers must not only be critical, but they must also be cautious in accepting as proven findings which have not been *repeated*. Ideally, findings should be repeated several times, by several different researchers with different samples of subjects, before being accepted as reliable.

Listed below are some of the points which readers should look for in deciding whether the findings of a particular piece of research are reliable or not.

(à) Does the researcher say how the autistic children he is testing have been diagnosed?

(b) Does the research report state other descriptive details of the children tested, such as their age, sex, intellectual level, and any other data which may be relevant to the findings? For example, in a study of social behaviour, it might be relevant to know whether the children were institutionalised or living at home; in a study where speed of response is measured it would be relevant to know whether any of the children were receiving medication such as, for example, phenobarbitone for the control of epileptic fits. Failure to provide all the relevant information can make the interpretation of research findings difficult, and undermine the value of research.

(c) If the research uses control groups, has the researcher chosen suitable groups as control? Control groups are used in order to make comparisons, and comparisons are made to identify specific abnormalities. Suppose, for example, that a research worker wants to know whether autistic children's speed of reaction is abnormal. If he compares autistic children with a control group composed of normal children of the same ages as the autistic children he is testing, and finds that autistic children react more slowly than controls, he has shown nothing unexpected or distinctive about autism, since most autistic children (as defined in this chapter) are subnormal in intelligence, and subnormal children, whether autistic or not, react on average more slowly than normal children. A suitable control group in this case would be a group of children matched with the autistic group for intelligence. If autistic children react more slowly than other (non-autistic) subnormals, then the research has shown something that may be a distinctive feature of autism.

To take another example, since it is one which recurs in research with autistic children; if any piece of research with autistic children involves the use of language, a suitable control group must be one which is as retarded in language as the autistic children who are tested. This is true whether (i) the child is *told* what he must do in the test (he will understand spoken instructions less well than children with better developed language); (ii) the test itself actually involves spoken or written language (for example, if children are asked to 'Show me the red square'); (iii) the test involves the kind of *thinking* for which we normally use language (for example, if a child is asked to lay down coloured counters in a row just like one he saw half a minute ago; this task is usually solved by the child memorising 'blue, purple, black, pink, red' or such-like, and is more difficult to do without using the colour names).

(d) If treatment methods are being compared, is each method given an equal chance of proving itself successful? For example, if two groups of children are treated by two different methods, are the two groups similar in all important respects? If they are not, the fact that one group responds to treatment better than the other may have nothing to do with the dif-

143

ferent treatment methods used, but stem simply from one group being, for instance, more intelligent than the other. Similarly, if two educational methods are compared, using different sets of teachers, it is important to ensure as far as possible that neither set of teachers is better informed, more experienced, more enthusiastic, than the other set.

(e) If the researcher has drawn a conclusion from his findings is the conclusion the correct one? If not, should some different conclusion be drawn, or should the conclusion be left open? For example, if autistic children react to stimulation more slowly than other subnormal children, would it be correct to conclude that their muscles are less well co-ordinated? Or might they have reacted slowly because they were not motivated to react; or because they had not understood what they were meant to do? Did the researchers exclude these and other possibilities before coming to a conclusion of poor co-ordination?

Most research reports are brief, being five to ten pages long on average. The *Journal of Autism and Childhood Schizophrenia* is partly devoted to work about autistic children and contains many original research reports. Reference lists at the end of such papers allow the reader to explore particular aspects of the reported work. Most university or school of education libraries either have in stock or can obtain journals or reprints of particular articles.

RESEARCH FINDINGS

1 Different approaches to teaching autistic children

The psychodynamic approach

This approach to treatment views autism as a condition with predominantly emotional rather than learned or physical origin. Psychodynamic writers on autism such as Bettelheim (1967) are interested in the internal conflict of the psyche; very roughly speaking, this approach is one which may be traced back to the work of Freud.

The superb early descriptions of autistic children in the psychodynamic literature are unfortunately not paralleled by adequate research reports on these children. Though the humanitarian attitudes and unstinting care of those using a psychodynamic approach is undoubted, it is hard to find research which supports the claims made for this approach, either in terms of the theory underlying psychodynamic treatment and teaching techniques, or in terms of the success of the techniques themselves.

A pernicious aspect of psychodynamic theorising has been to aggravate the parents' existing feelings of guilt by blaming them for the withdrawal of the autistic child from normal human contact. Ascription of blame in this respect appears from research to be, in fact, unjustified. Investigations by Creak and Ini (1960) and Pitfield and Oppenheim (1964), for example, make it clear that parents of autistic children are a random sample of ordinary people in their attitudes and child-rearing practices. Cox et al. (1975) suggest that it is the child's abnormality which produces stress in the form of anxiety and depression in the parents, rather than the interaction between the child and parent occurring the other way about. This is the classical parental reaction to any child with a severe chronically handicapping condition (Wing, 1976a and b).

Behaviour modification

Behaviour modification techniques are based on the learning theories of academic psychologists such as B. F. Skinner. Some theorists (for example, Ferster, 1961) attempted to explain autism in terms of abnormal learning associated with deviant parental care. Such explanations are not now thought to be convincing. However, the practical work generated by principles derived from learning theory is more impressive. Papers by Lovaas et al. (1974) and Evans (1971) give good accounts of this approach to treatment and teaching.

Behaviour modification focuses on observed behaviour rather than hypothetical underlying processes. Analysis of the individual's behaviour and how he responds to the rewards or 'punishments' (pleasant and unpleasant experiences) which he experiences in his environment is the keystone of this approach (Ross, 1974). For example, Evans in his paper (1971) describes an analysis of the symptom of mutism, i.e. failure to speak, in two children. He points out that only careful observation differentiated the child who was *unable* to speak from the child who could speak but who *chose not to*. In the former situation the child needed to be taught the basic skills of speaking, and in the other the child needed to be systematically rewarded for any attempts at the *social* use of speech. Jones *et al.* (1974) described how, to reduce self-injury which a severely autistic girl inflicted on herself, therapists used mild electric shock which was administered whenever self-injuring behaviour began. The therapists noted that, contrary to their expectations, the shock increased rather than decreased this girl's self-destructive behaviour. They concluded that this particular child either found electric shock rewarding, or else the attention that was being paid to her behaviour was satisfying despite the shock which was involved. Going on from this they found that failure to pay the child attention by isolating her in a deserted room when self-destructive behaviour occurred was effective in reducing it. The principle of this course of action is called time out from reinforcement, and has been reported as a useful technique for fading out undesirable behaviour in other cases of autism (Churchill, 1969).

In phasing out problem behaviours in autistic children there is a constant need to search for behaviours of a more appropriate kind to fill the 'available behaviour space'. Thus, whilst reducing reinforcement of inappropriate behaviours the therapist or teacher *must* be alert to the increasing need to reinforce appropriate behaviours (Lovaas *et al.*, 1974; Hewett, 1965). It may be necessary to start with so-called primary reinforcers like food which may be used to establish particular behaviours. Such reinforcers are most effective when the child has not eaten for a little time. It is sometimes claimed that autistic children are not, as a group, fond of sweets. If behaviour modification is being attempted, clearly it will be important to determine what any particular child finds rewarding in the way of food. Primary reinforcers may later be paired with secondary reinforcers like praise or attention, but such pairing may be very difficult to establish.

Setting up the therapy situation carefully as a 'positive reinforcer', or as rewarding in itself, is emphasised by Evans. Dealing with an echolalic girl he found that some therapy sessions were totally disorganised by her echoing, whereas in others she learned to produce much more appropriate speech. On examining what happened in the social situation *before* the therapy sessions, it was found that when the girl was involved in activities which she enjoyed, and the therapy training sessions interrupted this enjoyable activity, an unsuccessful treatment session ensued. When on the other hand the girl came to the therapy room from stressful situations which she disliked, a successful treatment session was achieved. Clearly this child's ability to benefit from therapy was determined by whether she perceived the session as an unpleasant interruption, or as a welcome relief from aversive activity.

The establishing of a new behaviour in autistic children is often much more difficult than the elimination of disturbed behaviour (Risley and Wolf, 1967). This might be due to inherent limitations in the capacity to learn (Hingten and Churchill, 1969), or to the poor motivation and negativism which is often said to be characteristic of these children (Cowan, Hoddinott and Wright, 1965). Emotional reactivity is certainly a factor contributing to the autistic child's difficulty in learning: Churchill (1971) showed that failure even of a trivial kind can disorganise the autistic child's behaviour for long periods. Thus programmes for introducing new behaviours must be planned in finely graded steps each of which the child has good chance of achieving successfully. By such a technique of 'successive approximations' the child's spontaneous responses can be gradually developed or shaped. For example, basic unstructured sound can be developed into understandable words by rewarding increases in accuracy of imitation of the therapist's speech (Lovaas *et al.*, 1974).

The use of punishment is an emotive issue in the treatment of autistic children. It is probably distasteful to the teacher to find references in the research literature to the use of electric shock or punishment, but the use of punishment must be set against the frightening results of unchecked behaviour. Wing (1967a and b), for example, refers to two children who produced severe damage to their vision by self-mutilating behaviour. The questions which need to be asked are: 'Is there any other method of reducing this behaviour?' and 'Will this child be more injured by the original behaviour or the "punishment"?' Punishment has been shown to suppress, but

147

not to remove, deviant behaviour in children (Skinner, 1957). Thus, as soon as the punishment ceases, the behaviour is likely to recur, given an appropriate 'trigger'; however, this can be prevented by teaching new behaviour which is incompatible with the performance of the original unwanted behaviour.

Behaviour modification techniques are time-consuming, producing small gains for major efforts (Lovaas *et al.*, 1974). They are most successful where the environment is controllable and most of the research literature to date shows best results from this programme applied to specific (often minor) aspects of behaviour in a laboratory or specially constructed environment (Evans, 1971). However, behaviour therapists report, as a result of objective research studies, that some improvement can be made in nearly all cases, using these methods. Moreover, they have shown that their methods, although time-consuming, can be efficiently carried out by parents, teachers, or helpers with very little training, and that behaviour modification can in some instances be used in small groups of children which is, of course, more economical of teacher time than is individual training.

Perhaps the greatest criticism of the usefulness of behaviour modification techniques is the frequent failure of behaviour acquired in one situation (such as a specific classroom situation) to generalise, or carry over, to other similar but not identical situations. Thus, if a child achieves a certain skill, e.g. the ability to speak a few words appropriately, there is no guarantee that this ability will increase in the home or school situation unless reinforcement of this behaviour is continued and the repertoire extended by systematic individual teaching both at home and at school. This problem is being researched by Schopler *et al.* (1971), who feel that involving parents in these programmes will cause a greater consistency in the application of these techniques and therefore greater (and more stable) gains for the children.

Environmental approaches

Papers on the perceptual processes of autistic children suggest that they have difficulties in perceiving patterns, or regularities in the things they experience (Rutter, 1974). Thus, they find it hard to make sense of, or to feel sure of, what is coming to them from outside. The autistic child appears to crave 'sameness' in his life (Kanner, 1943), and to impose a rigid stereotyped way of responding to external stimuli (Hermelin and Frith, 1971) and probably to internal processes. Security for the autistic child appears to reside in the predictability of his environment. It is in this sense that research reports refer to what is called 'a structured environment'. The word 'structure' does not imply rigid scheduling of a child in an uncaring environment, but adult-determined, task-directed activities organised to suit the needs of the particular child or, more commonly, small group of children.

The use of structured environments in teaching autistic children is an approach which has been evolved, not by theorists or researchers, but by those actually working in special schools for autistic children. An interesting account of the development of one example of this kind of approach is given in a paper by Fenichel (1974), who was a director of a special school in America. Fenichel stresses the autistic child's need to have order and stability created for him. He writes:

> Our staff eventually came to accept discipline and structure not as negative concepts that meant rejecting, restricting or damaging a child, but as integral parts of a positive, corrective and therapeutic process. . . . The alternative was chaos, confusion.

Fenichel also stresses that discipline and structure should not preclude the child's free expression of his emotions, though they may guide and check that expression. He speaks of the need for sensitivity and insight in teachers, and the need for teachers to be able to identify with the child's conflicts and emotions. Thus, the structured approach draws together elements from both the psychodynamic and the behaviourist approaches to working with autistic children. An insistence on the need for consistency and regularity in the child's environment, and the use of discipline, are characteristic of the behaviourist approach; whereas the emphasis on the need to consider the child as a dynamic whole, and stress on the importance of interpersonal relationships are particularly characteristic of the psychodynamic approach.

149

The relative effectiveness of the three different approaches

Not enough research has been done to enable a decision to be made as to which of the available approaches to the treatment and education of autistic children—the psychodynamic approach, behaviour modification or the use of structured environments—has most to recommend it. However, a few research studies have been reported which have attempted to compare the success of the different methods.

In a study by Schopler *et al.* (1971) for example, the effects of permissive (child-directed) and structured (adult-directed) environments were assessed. Structured treatment sessions brought about greater improvement than unstructured sessions in the children's emotionality, the amount of psychotic behaviour which occurred, the amount of vocalisation which the children used, and the degree to which they related to other people. Unstructured sessions, in which the child was left to direct his own activities although cared for by an adult, produced some improvement in more able autistic children, but very little change in the behaviour of the less able children.

In another study (Rutter and Bartak, 1973), autistic children's progress in three different schools, ranging from the permissive to the highly structured in approach, was compared. The children in all three schools showed very similar improvements in social and linguistic behaviour over a period of years. Scholastic progress was greatest in children attending the school whose programme and approach were highly structured. This was not surprising, however, in view of the greater emphasis placed on formal education in this school than in either of the others.

In another study in which the progress of children in different kinds of schools or institutions was compared (Wenar *et al.*, 1967), the most psychodynamically oriented and permissive environment produced most improvement in the children. However, in this study other institutions which were examined provided in one case only custodial care, and in another planned therapeutic activities 'executed with indifference'. The essential ingredient which gave the psychodynamic school greater success than the two other institutions may, therefore, very likely have been the quality of relationships which were made with the children, rather than the use of specifically psychotherapeutic teaching/treatment methods.

In a study by Ney *et al.* (1971) the results of treatment using play therapy, and treatment using behaviour modification were compared. Both treatment methods were found to bring about improvements in the children's non-verbal and verbal skills. However, behaviour modification produced significantly better results than play therapy when the methods were assessed over quite a long period of time.

From such studies as those above it may be tentatively concluded (a) that establishing a good relationship is an important prerequisite of successful work with an autistic child, and schools which offer individualised care produce improvements in social-emotional development and language skills. However, (b) structured environments and behaviour therapy can, at least in some situations, produce more improvement in certain areas of development than does play therapy, or an unstructured 'permissive' approach.

2 Autistic children's behaviour

In this section some research findings on autistic children's emotional and cognitive, or 'thinking', processes are described. To illustrate the complexity of the skills involved in apparently simple tasks, consider what is involved if the child is shown three coloured shapes — a red circle, a red square and a blue square — and is asked by the teacher, 'Which is the red square?' At least all of the following skills will be needed:

(a) *attentiveness*—being alert to listen and to do what is required;

(b) *hearing* and *understanding* the instruction;

(c) *remembering* what has been said for long enough to carry out the instruction;

(d) *seeing* and *attending*—first to the coloured shapes (rather than to the table top or other nearby objects); second, to colour and shape (rather than to size or position of the shapes on the table, or relative to each other);

(e) *association*—of what has been heard with what can be seen.

151

There is some evidence that autistic children's behaviour is to some extent abnormal in all of the processes listed above. Not all autistic children have abnormalities in all these processes, but a majority have been found to be abnormal in some or all of these respects. Some of the kinds of difficulties which have been found to exist are described below.

Attentiveness and arousal

To be attentive (that is, able to concentrate on what he is doing), a child must be alert, not 'switched off'. On the other hand he must not be too excited or 'high', or he will be easily distracted by any disturbance or counter-attraction, and thus emotionally unstable and not in full control of his behaviour. Autistic children who are over-excited in this way make odd noises such as moaning, whining or roaring. Typically, they also make whatever repetitive movements are habitual to them (such as rolling their heads from side to side, flapping their hands, biting or hitting themselves). These noises and movements become more vigorous, intense, and more rapidly executed if the level of excitement increases.

Levels of excitability or 'arousal' vary greatly in autistic children. Each autistic child at each stage of development has an average level of excitability (ranging from the very high to the very low), around which he fluctuates in an unstable way. So conspicuous are the abnormalities of excitement levels in autistic children, that two theories were put forward during the 1960s which suggested that abnormal arousal is the root cause of the whole syndrome. As noted in chapter 2, one of these theories, proposed by Rimland (1964), suggested that autistic children are chronically *under*-aroused (unresponsive), and the other, put forward by Hutt *et al.* (1965), suggested that autistic children are chronically *over*-aroused; although nobody has carried out all the research that would be needed to get to the truth of this matter, there is evidence from electroencephalograms, and from studies of arousal behaviour, which indicates that both theories have some truth in them, and that the real difficulty may therefore be seen as lying in the *control* of arousal. It has already been mentioned that autistic children may over-react in an excited way to the experience of failure. It is also noted (Furneaux, personal communication) that autistic children may over-react to success or praise. It is, moreover, typical of autistic children to *over*-react to sound on some occasions, but to *under*-react on others. Observations such as these could be explained in terms of poorly controlled levels of excitability; for example, even normal people may be startled by a small sound if tense, but fail to hear a much louder sound if relaxed. Whatever the cause of the autistic child's characteristics in excitability, it may be useful for those working with autistic children to remember that one and the same child may at one time be startled by a sudden movement, but at another may need the stimulus of a sudden movement, or sharp sound, to arouse their attention.

Another theory concerning autistic children's emotional reactions suggests that these children react excessively and abnormally to social approaches made by other people. Richer (1974), who puts forward this theory, has made videotapes of autistic children with their teachers, showing the children turning their heads away, becoming upset, and starting to perform stereotyped movements if a teacher comes too close, raises her voice above a certain level, or stares into the child's face. As Richer points out, when a child turns away and will not co-operate, the normal reaction of the teacher is to become more demanding in her voice and manner. Richer suggests that this may actually be counter-productive, and that a more useful strategy might be for the teacher to look away and remain quiet until abnormal arousal subsides and the child is able to be attentive again. However, Richer also mentions that, although *moderate* social intrusions into the child's world may provoke arousal and escape reactions, *very strong* intrusions (actually shouting, or catching hold of the child, for example) can also be effective in breaking into an escalating spiral of excitability—rather as a splash of cold water, or slap on the face, can stop 'hysterics'. Another factor to be borne in mind when considering how to approach an autistic child to get his attentive co-operation, concerns how well the child knows a particular adult. Contrary to general belief, some autistic children enjoy being cuddled by an adult whom they

153

know well. A light touch from a stranger can, by contrast, cause them to shrink away.

Understanding and memory

Autistic children do not learn language easily, if at all. Theorists differ as to why this should be the case, even in those children who may show peaks of high non-verbal ability. Bettelheim, for instance, whose psychodynamic theory of autism has already been mentioned, believes that emotional and personality disturbance is at the root of the child's failure to learn language. Richer considers that it may be the autistic child's fear of social situations which causes him to retreat from both relating and communicating.

Nowadays, this kind of view—that is, that the autistic child does not communicate because he is severely withdrawn and unable to relate to people—is something of a minority view. The more common view in recent years has been to look for cognitive difficulties (that is, impairment in the intellectual, or thinking process) which might make it difficult for the autistic child to acquire language.

One suggested cognitive abnormality has been investigated by Hermelin and O'Connor (Hermelin and O'Connor, 1970; Hermelin, 1976) and Frith (1970) in a number of interesting experiments. In most of Hermelin, O'Connor and Frith's experiments lists of words, or sentences, were spoken aloud and the child was asked to repeat what he had heard. On the principle that 'what does not come out has not gone in' the experimenters then looked at the children's attempts at repetition, and drew conclusions about what the children 'registered' when things were said to them. The conclusion reached by Hermelin, O'Connor and Frith was that autistic children probably register *sounds* rather than *meaning*, and that the sounds are stored in memory in an unanalysed form—that is, more or less exactly as they were heard. Normal people usually register meaning more than sounds (unless for example, listening to a foreign language, or trying to pick out a familiar voice from a crowd of others). The normal person then analyses the meaning of what he has heard and stores it in a condensed form, filed, as it were, under certain relevant headings. If autistic children register sounds rather than meaning, and if they do not analyse and condense what they hear, it follows that they will not easily learn spoken language, nor understand — nor understand — nor remember — long or complicated things which are said to them.

If Hermelin *et al.*'s conclusions are correct, teachers might want to think about ways of communicating with autistic children without the use of sound. Unfortunately, however, it seems likely from experiments testing autistic children's use of gesture and their ability to understand what they read (Bartak *et al.*, 1975), that visual systems of communication are not very efficient either. Any practical courses of action following on from Hermelin, O'Connor and Frith's conclusions are therefore depressingly difficult to point to.

However, it also seems possible that Hermelin *et al.*'s findings could be explained in quite another way. For 'what does not come out' may have gone in, but then have been lost or forgotten; that is to say, information may be registered in the memory store but may not be retrievable from it. Some experiments by Boucher and Warrington (1976) indicate that this could be what happens when autistic children are asked to repeat lists of words, or sentences. In these experiments it was shown that autistic children are very poor at remembering if they are given no help at all, but if they are given some help at remembering (for example, the first sound of a word, such as 'b' for 'baby', or a clue as to meaning such as 'an animal' for 'cow') most autistic children can remember what has been said to them not only as well as other handicapped children, but as well as normal children of their own age. This suggests that autistic children may register and store information normally, but are unable to recall it to mind in the normal way. DeMyer (1971), reporting some experiments on autistic children's ability to imitate actions, comes to a similar conclusion. She found that autistic children are poor at imitation unless they have some unambiguous clue as to 'how to begin'; then they may imitate the action quite normally.

Autistic children have in some respects strikingly good memories, especially for things such as the words of a song, or a list of the kings of England, which have been rote-learned. So the question of whether autistic children have impaired

155

memory is not a simple one. However, if it were proved beyond doubt that in some kinds of learning and memorising the provision of a clue can make all the difference between success and failure, this knowledge might be very useful to teachers. It could also possibly explain one of the things teachers find exasperating about autistic children: namely, the way they seem to know a thing one day and not the next. For it may be that the precise way of asking a question either provides, or fails to provide, the clue the child needs in order to remember the answer to a question he is asked. For example, the question, 'What did you do at the weekend?' provides no clues, whereas the question, 'Did you go shopping with Mummy at the weekend?' may enable the child to remember details of a shopping expedition which he might not otherwise be able to recall.

Attention

In recent years a number of pieces of research have been published (see, for example, Koegel and Wilhelm, 1973), which suggest that autistic children's 'selective attention' processes are abnormal in certain ways. The phrase 'selective attention' needs some explanation. If we attended to everything that passed before our eyes, under our noses and into our ears, we would, in effect, be swamped with unusable information. Moreover, we would not be able to acquire concepts, since concept formation requires that the individual selectively attends to the similarities, and ignores the differences, between things. All cats resemble each other in having four legs, whiskers, green eyes, and soft fur; the fact that one cat is ginger and another tabby, and one is fat and another thin, is irrelevant to the concept of a cat. In the example of asking the child, 'Which is the red square', the only way to get the answer consistently right is to attend selectively to colour and to shape, and to ignore the size, texture, position, etc. of the coloured shapes.

Experiments on selective attention processes in autistic children suggest that these children may attend *over-selectively*: for example, they might focus on colour and ignore shape, and thus not be able to distinguish the red circle from the red square. Or they might think that what made cats 'cats' was the fact that they have whiskers (ignoring number of legs, colour of eyes, sounds made, etc.) in which case the distinction between cats and other animals with whiskers will not be made. In the experiment by Koegel and Wilhelm, for example, twelve out of fifteen autistic children attended only to the position in which the stimuli were presented, and ignored size and shape; whereas twelve out of fifteen normal children attended to all the characteristics of the presented material in making their comparisons.

Not only does such research suggest that autistic children notice *fewer* characteristics of things about them than do other children, it also appears that autistic children notice unusual characteristics, and not necessarily the sort of things that normal people notice. For example, they are often observed to solve jigsaw puzzles quite as readily when the pieces are face down, as when the pieces are face up. An experiment by Boucher (in preparation) indicates that this is because, when both *shape* characteristics and *pictorial* characteristics can be used to solve a puzzle, autistic children only notice the shapes of the pieces, whereas normal children after a certain age take more notice of the picture the pieces make than they do of the shape, but pay some attention to both characteristics. Interestingly, when no shape clues were available, autistic children showed themselves well able to attend to pictorial meaning in order to solve the puzzle.

Other instances of autistic children selectively attending to unusual aspects of things around them occur in several experiments which are reported by Hermelin and O'Connor (1970). These authors showed that touch and movement are peculiarly important to autistic children. If a buzzer was sounded and simultaneously a small tug was given on a piece of string tied round the child's ankle, autistic children, unlike other children tested, were more likely to attend to the thing they felt than the thing they heard. Similarly, when lights and sounds were presented simultaneously from different parts of the room, autistic children tended to look towards the same part of the room each time, rather than responding consistently to lights, or consistently to sounds, as other children tended to do. It appears that the autistic child concentrates on place, and the feel of a particular movement such as turning

157

towards a particular place, and does not notice audible and visible things so readily.

What might be the applications to teaching of this rather curious set of observations on selective attention? Since the findings are far from giving a complete picture of how the world looks, sounds and feels to an autistic child, compared with our selective pictures of the world, perhaps the main point to stress is that teachers should never assume that the autistic child is attending to the same things as they are. The autistic child's attention may have to be directed to a specific feature which he is required to pay attention to. If necessary, all other 'distracting' (irrelevant) features which he might more naturally attend to (such as the position of objects, relative to the child) may have to be removed, or his attention drawn away from them. On the positive side, the findings confirm the suggestion frequently made by teachers and others, that autistic children 'learn by doing', and may benefit at certain stages of development from teaching methods based on tactile and kinaesthetic sensation (Furneaux, 1969).

Association

Fundamental to the normal person's ability to make sense of the world, and particularly to his ability to build up a system of complex concepts, and to learn verbal labels for those concepts, is the capacity to associate together what is perceived by all the different senses. Thus, a fire is seen as red and felt as hot; a clock is seen to have a face and hands, and heard to tick. The words 'fire' and 'clock' are associated with complex memories of things seen, smelt, touched, heard and tasted.

There is some evidence from research that some autistic children do not make these fundamental associations in the normal way. In particular, there is evidence to suggest that words which are heard are not readily associated with what the child perceives through his other senses. A research paper by Bryson (1970) is a useful one to read for information about autistic children's possible difficulties in what is sometimes called 'cross modal coding'. (A 'mode' as used here simply means one of the senses; 'cross modal association' means associating together information from the different sense channels; 'cross modal coding' means having a verbal label or other kind of 'name' or sign, for a set of cross modal associations.) The possibility that some autistic children have deficits of this kind is important because of the devastating effect such difficulties could have on a child's ability to acquire concepts and language of any sort, whether spoken, written or signed, and because the possibility might be a useful one for teachers to bear in mind when faced with some of the autistic child's less explicable learning failures. However, research in this area is incomplete, and as is the case with all the areas of research which have been mentioned in this chapter, much more needs to be done before researchers can say confidently 'this is how it is' and teachers can say 'therefore we will use this particular teaching method with this particular child'.

Summary

In this chapter some research findings which could be relevant to the teaching of autistic children are described. Findings are divided into two categories: (1) those concerned with different overall treatment of autistic children (the psychodynamic approach, the behaviourist approach, and the use of structured environments); (2) those concerned with autistic children's behaviour. Some points are also made concerning the critical evaluation of research findings.

References

Bartak, L., Rutter, M. and Cox, A. (1975) 'A comparative study of infantile autism and specific developmental receptive language disorder: I. The children', *Brit. J. Psychiat.*, 126, pp. 127–45.

Bettelheim, B. (1967) *The Empty Fortress: Infantile Autism and the Birth of the Self*, Free Press, New York.

Boucher, J. M. and Warrington, E. (1976) 'Memory deficits in early infantile autism: some similarities to the amnesic syndrome', *Brit. J. Psychol.*, 67.

Bryson, C. Q. (1970) 'Systematic identification of perceptual difficulties in autistic children', *Percep. Motor Skills*, 31, pp. 239–46.

Churchill, D. (1969) 'Psychotic children and behaviour modification', *American Journal of Psychiatry*, 125, pp. 1585–90.

Churchill, D. W. (1971) 'Effects of success and failure in psychotic children', *Arch. Gen. Psychiat.*, 25, pp. 208–14.

Cowan, P. A., Hoddinott, B. A. and Wright, B. A. (1965) 'Compliance and resistance in the conditioning of autistic children: an exploratory study', *Child Development*, 36, pp. 212–33.

Cox, A., Rutter, M., Newman, S. and Bartak, L. (1975) 'A comparative study of infantile autism and specific developmental language disorders: II. Parental characteristics', *Brit. J. Psychiat.*, 126, 146–59.

Creak, M. and Ini, S. (1960) 'Families of psychotic children', *J. Child Psychol. Psychiat.*, 1, p. 156.

DeMyer, M. K. (1971) 'Perceptual limitations in autistic children and their relation to social and intellectual deficits', in M. Rutter (ed.), *Infantile Autism: Concepts, Characteristics and Treatment*, Churchill, London.

Evans, I. A. (1971) 'Theoretical and experimental aspects of the behaviour modification to autistic children', in M. Rutter (ed.), *Infantile Autism: Concepts, Characteristics and Treatment*, Churchill, London.

Fenichel, C. (1974) 'Special education as a basic therapeutic tool', *J. Aut. Child Schiz.*, 4, pp. 177–96.

Ferster, C. B. (1961) 'Positive reinforcement and behavioural deficits of autistic children', *Child Development*, 32, pp. 437–56.

Frith, U. (1970) 'Studies in pattern detection in normal and autistic children: I. Immediate recall of auditory sequences', *J. Ab. Psychol*, 76, pp. 413–20.

Furneaux, B. (1969) *The Special Child*, Penguin Education Special, Harmondsworth.

Hermelin, B. (1976) 'Coding and the sense modalities', in J. K. Wing (ed.), *Early Childhood Autism*, Pergamon, Oxford.

Hermelin, B. and Frith, U. (1971) 'Psychological studies of childhood autism: Can autistic children make sense of what they see and hear?', *Journal of Special Education*, 50, pp. 107–17.

Hermelin, B. and O'Connor, N. (1970) *Psychological Experiments with Autistic Children*, Pergamon, Oxford.

Hewett, F. M. (1965) 'Teaching speech to an autistic child through operant conditioning', *Amer. J. Orthopsychiat.*, 35, pp. 927–36.

Hingten, J. N. and Churchill, D. W. (1969) 'Identification of perceptual limitations in mute autistic children', *Arch. Gen. Psychiat.*, 21, pp. 68–81.

Hutt, S. J., Hutt, C., Lee, D. and Ounsted, C. (1965) 'A behavioural and electroencephalographic study of autistic children', *J. Psychiat. Res.*, 3, pp. 181–97.

Jones, F. H., Simmons, J. Q. and Frankel, F. (1974) 'An extinction procedure for eliminating self-destructive behaviour in a 9-year-old autistic girl', *J. Aut. Child. Schiz.*, 4, pp. 241–50.

Kanner, L. (1943) 'Autistic disturbances of affective contact', *Nervous Child*, 2, pp. 217–50.

Koegel, R. L. and Wilhelm, H. (1973) 'Selective responding to the components of multiple visual cues by autistic children', *J. Exp. Child. Psychol.*, 15, pp. 442–53.

Lovaas, O. I. (1966) 'A program for the establishment of speech in psychotic children', in J. K. Wing (ed.), *Early Childhood Autism*, Pergamon, Oxford, pp. 115–44.

Lovaas, O. I., Schreibman, L. and Koegel, R. L. (1974) 'A behaviour modification approach to the treatment of autistic children', *J. Aut. Child. Schiz.*, 4; 2, pp. 111–29.

Ney, P. G., Palvesky, A. E. and Markely, J. (1971) 'Relative effectiveness of operant conditioning and play therapy in childhood schizophrenia', *J. Aut. Child. Schiz.*, 1, pp. 337–49.

Pitfield, M. and Oppenheim, A. N. (1964) 'Child-rearing attitudes of mothers of psychotic children', *J. Child. Psychol. Psychiat.*, 5, p. 51.

Richer, J. (1974) 'The Social and Stereotyped Behaviour of Autistic Children', unpublished doctoral thesis, Reading University.

Rimland, B. (1964) *Infantile Autism*, Appleton-Century-Crofts, New York.

Risley, T. R. and Wolf, M. M. (1967) 'Establishing functional speech in echolalic children', *Behaviour, Research and Therapy*, 5, pp. 73–88.

Ross, A. O. (1974) *Psychological Disorders of Children. A Behavioural Approach to Theory, Research and Therapy*, McGraw-Hill, New York.

Rutter, M. (1968) 'Concepts of autism: a review of research', *J. Child Psychol. Psychiat.*, 9, pp. 1–25.

Rutter, M. (1974) 'The development of infantile autism', *Psychological Medicine*, 4, pp. 147–63.

Rutter, M. and Bartak, L. (1973) 'Special educational treatment of autistic children: a comparative study', *J. Child Psych. and Psychiat.*, 14, pp. 161–79 and 241–70.

Schopler, E., Reichler, R. J., Brehm, S. and Kinsbourne, M. (1971) 'The effect of treatment structure on development in autistic children', *Arch. Gen. Psychiat.*, 24, pp. 415–21.

Skinner, B. F. (1957) quoted in B. F. Skinner, *Freedom and Dignity*, Penguin, Harmondsworth, p. 64.

Wenar, C. W., Ruttenberg, B. A., Dratman, M. L. and Wolf, E. G. (1967) 'Changing autistic behaviour', *Arch. Gen. Psychiat.*, 17, pp. 26–35.

Wing, L. (1976a) 'Diagnosis, clinical description and prognosis', in L. Wing (ed.), *Early Childhood Autism*, Pergamon, Oxford.

Wing, L. (1976b) 'Epidemiology and theories of aetiology', in L. Wing (ed.), *Early Childhood Autism*, Pergamon, Oxford.

8 The specialist advisory services

JEANNE HERTZOG

Clive was 5 and new to primary school when a medical officer called in his classroom, at the request of his teacher, and observed his odd behaviour. Soon afterwards Clive's parents were asked to come and discuss with the Headteacher something which they feared, knew that they had observed, but were reluctant to admit existed. For some months his behaviour had been unusual, especially when he thought he was alone; in a play situation he could be seen mimicking a flying movement, jumping up and down and 'flapping' his arms for surprisingly long periods, his apparently alert and attractive face looking tense and drawn. This could continue as an exclusive activity for an hour or more at a time and attempts to divert his attention were useless.

The medical officer decided to request the help of the school psychological service and in her letter of referral she commented that Clive's speech was very limited and that he showed some signs of general retardation. The psychologist saw Clive and then asked the psychiatrist at the same Child Guidance Clinic to investigate him for her. Then followed in swift succession the boy's assessment and subsequent admission to a school specialising in the diagnosis and teaching of autistic children, side by side with others who are behaviourally disturbed. Clive was now with the consent of his parents (who had been consulted throughout) going to be taught in a highly specialised atmosphere geared to his individual needs. His first class teacher, the school medical officer, a psychologist and, finally, a psychiatrist had combined their efforts to find the most appropriate placement for him.

No discussion of the education of autistic children would be complete if it failed to consider the vital role which the special-

162

ist and advisory services play in the overall care of the child and his family. Frequently these individuals from the various disciplines of medicine, psychology, nursing, social work, etc. are the first to be involved with the child and his parents. It is they who identify the children with special needs, and who first support and advise the family; it is they who suggest that a child may require special education and, having gained the parents' confidence and agreement, try to arrange the most appropriate school placement.

The main specialists who are normally concerned are the psychiatrist, the paediatrician, the local medical officer, the psychologist and either the health visitor or a social worker. Others who could be involved at different stages include the neurologist, the consultant in encephalography (the doctor who interprets brainwave recordings), the audiologist, the speech therapist and even the dentist and the ENT surgeon. Each specialist has a separate role to play although individually they may at times seem to be offering a service similar to that of a colleague in a different speciality. In fact this is not usually the case; they are contributing their particular skills so that the most complete information possible can be brought to bear upon the child and his problems. For example, the psychiatrist, the paediatrician, the neurologist and the psychologist could all have a diagnostic function; but each one might also be included in the treatment of the child. The audiologist and the speech therapist may need to investigate special aspects of the patient's problem and establish certain facts, but again they both (but more frequently the speech therapist) could be involved in treatment. The same holds true to a lesser extent in relation to the EEG specialist, the neurologist, the dentist and the ENT surgeon, but since their roles are so clearly defined this will not be discussed here.

Jennifer was the first child of young and inexperienced parents. Clinically the pregnancy was uneventful with labour lasting a mere five hours from the first pains to the actual birth. When mother and baby returned home from hospital, the parents began to think how fortunate they were; she was so undemanding that, as the mother put it 'no one knew we had a baby in the house'. She reported that Jennifer did not cry when a feed was due and seemed to be content and totally self-sufficient. She would lie for hours apparently absorbed in watching the movements of her own hands or, if in her pram in the garden, the leaves above her head. She showed no wish to be picked up or cuddled. In fact, she tended to stiffen and put her arm between herself and anyone who attempted to lift her. However, her parents were not unduly worried; the fact that Jennifer was so undemanding left her mother free to carry out what were to her the unfamiliar chores of running a home. Jennifer sat up at the usual time, crawled at eight months and was walking soon after her first birthday.

As she appeared to need so little attention, Jennifer's parents tended to offer nothing apart from routine caring. It was clear that their little daughter was never in distress so, although they loved her dearly, they felt relaxed enough to occupy themselves with other concerns, though at times the mother wished Jennifer was more affectionate. In spite of the fact that she rejected being cuddled and failed to smile responsively, it appeared reasonable in the first place that the mother should continue to be engrossed in household concerns, for, additionally, the health visitor who called regularly seemed to accept that all was well. It was only much later when they had a second child that Jennifer's parents came to realise that their first-born had never made her presence felt in the house. Watching and listening to the new baby they began to feel some alarm about Jennifer, but it was only when she failed to start talking that a truly deep anxiety set in. Jennifer was over 3 years old before the timid mother asked the health visitor for her opinion.

While the health visitor mentioned her own and the family's concern to the GP, the doctor at the baby clinic also became aware that the 3-year-old who accompanied mother and baby at each visit had not started to speak. When the mother told the clinic doctor that, among other things, Jennifer had never 'liked being cuddled' he promptly arranged a psychiatric referral. Within the next month a child psychiatrist had seen Jennifer and asked a psychologist to investigate further and referred her, after several sessions of close clinical observation, to a unit specialising in the diagnosis of autism. Jennifer was more fortunate than Clive; she had been referred well before school age to a group of concerned staff who could begin to help her so much sooner.

The teacher who chooses to teach autistic children is indeed taking on a very great challenge. The extent of uncertainty in this demanding field should be eased somewhat by the support of those advisory services which have played a part in assessing the child, where units are fortunate enough to have such facilities available. Nevertheless we have to bear in mind that children entering such a unit may still have a question mark over their heads in terms of the diagnosis. We have seen already the uncertain and diverse attitudes towards this particular condition and, earlier in this book, the way in which the teacher can play a part in trying to clarify the diagnosis in each individual case.

The many specialist and ancillary services which, as we have observed, contribute to the preparation of the child and his parents for the future as far as it can be determined, will now be discussed. (See Figure 8.1.)

1   The health visitor

Frequently the health visitor who visits a family with young children regularly may be the first person to discuss with the parents their anxiety regarding a child's slow development and odd behaviour. Health visitors, who are highly qualified nurses with training in midwifery and child health, are in many parts of the country attached to one particular general practice, so where this arrangement exists the health visitor will suggest that the parents consult the doctor from the group practice. She will at the same time describe her observations on the child's clinical state to the practitioner with whom she works.

Her part in the referral of the child may end at this point or later, when she may be invited to discuss her knowledge of the situation with the psychiatrist whom the GP has consulted, perhaps at an informal conference when a social worker is present. In many cases, however, she continues to be the friend and supporter of the family throughout all the stages of diagnosis and placement. Sometimes the pattern of referral may vary and a health visitor may suggest that a medical officer sees the child at the welfare clinic or, if the patient is

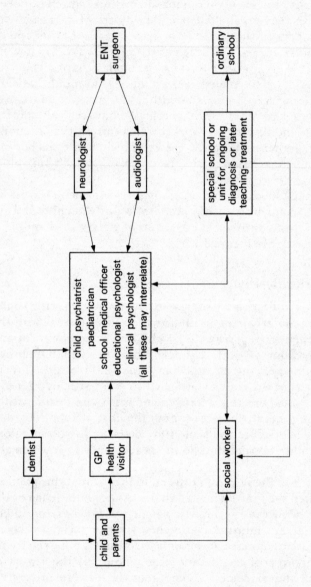

FIGURE 8.1 Possible referral and treatment 'routes' for a child considered to be autistic.

over the age of 5, at the school clinic. This alternative channel of referral can sometimes make help available more swiftly, but either route is entirely acceptable because the GP or the medical officer invariably seeks a paediatric or a psychiatric opinion.

2   The medical officer

Most medical officers work both in the schools and in the welfare clinic, thus seeing the children of school age at routine medical inspections, as well as infants and younger children in the clinic. Working as a member of the school health service this doctor, after examining a child who in his view could be autistic, may use the facilities of the school psychological service, asking the psychologist to give his opinion on the child's progress and potential. He may, however, delay such a request while he asks the audiologist to assess the child's hearing if he feels an assessment of this kind is indicated. The medical officer is aware that it is imperative to know the extent of any hearing loss in a child who is failing to respond to sounds or in whom speech is slow to develop.

Frequently, however, the medical officer will contact a medical colleague at a hospital or clinic. It will depend on the individual way in which the difficulties present themselves as to whether his choice for the next stage of investigations is the psychiatrist or the paediatrician. There is nearly always some overlap, and once more the specialist consultant will decide at what point to ask the psychologist for his opinion. The aim should be to establish that easy communication takes place at an early stage between the medical officer, the paediatrician, the psychiatrist and the psychologist with, subsequently, the combining of their views as to the next step to be taken. The smoothness with which these procedures are arranged—thus producing a feeling of confidence and reassurance in the parents—may well depend on the administrative skill and wise judgment of the medical officer.

That same wise judgment may again be called upon when the child becomes well enough to resume normal school. In this situation it is often the medical officer who prepares the way for the child's return partly through conversations with the local psychologist, or sometimes through direct talks with the Head of the school where the child has been placed. The doctor, who thus has full knowledge of the child's general stage, degree of progress, capacity for learning and basic needs is in an ideal position to impart this information to the Head and other teachers in the school to which the child is returning.

3 The paediatrician

In well over 50 per cent of the cases where a diagnosis of autism is in question, a paediatrician's opinion is sought by the GP, the medical officer or the psychiatrist. The paediatrician whose work is concerned with child health and children's diseases is more fully conversant than any other specialist with the norms relating to the child's development. In taking a history from the parents he will want full details of the child's 'milestones', i.e. the age at which the child started to speak simple words and then phrases, the age at which he began to walk and attain bladder and bowel control. He will also ask if the mother had any difficulties in pregnancy, whether the child sucked well at the breast or bottle and enquire into early feeding and sleeping patterns. Like the medical officer, the paediatrician will seek the opinion of the audiologist (if this has not been obtained) if the child's speech failed to develop normally. Even if such an investigation has been reported in the letter of referral he may still wish for a series of assessments to be carried out, since such children are difficult to test.

In discussing such specific questions as a history of difficult labour, childhood illnesses and accidents, the paediatrician will to some extent be overlapping the neurologist's sphere of concern, and when in fact parents give a history of difficulties connected with the nervous system, such as fits or head injury, it is likely that the paediatrician, whether or not he has found abnormalities in a physical examination, will want the child to be seen by a neurologist. This overlap professionally is very necessary especially if the paediatrician elicits in his clinical examination any signs that the nervous system may be damaged. He will as a routine have arranged blood and urine tests and, in particular, will have excluded the possibility of a disease called phenylketoneuria which inhibits a child's normal development.

Sometimes the paediatrician suspecting that there might be an area in the brain where cells have been damaged or destroyed (at birth or through illness or accident) will ask directly for an electroencephalogram to be carried out. This might lead occasionally to the by-passing of neurological help, but much more frequently the neurologist is asked for a diagnostic opinion and, before giving it, will himself request an EEG. Thus the paediatrician, the neurologist or even the psychiatrist may ask the consultant in EEG to comment on an EEG recording.

The paediatrician's role may end with the subsequent referral of a child to a psychiatrist or psychologist but in many instances requests will be made periodically for further evaluations of the child's state by his paediatric colleagues. This can prove an ongoing situation for many years, especially if doubt is still present with regard to diagnosis. The paediatrician remains in this way in contact with the child's development and can reassess his reaction to a change or changes in the environment and the general progress he has made.

4   The neurologist

The neurologist is the doctor who has studied in detail the nervous system in man, both in health and disease. His role is a very specific one as, by the time he examines the child, a differential diagnosis (a list of possible conditions causing the child's symptoms) will have been drawn up by the paediatrician, preceded by several other doctors, including the GP, or by the psychiatrist.

The paediatrician will already have carried out a full physical examination of the child, including the examination of the nervous system. The paediatrician may suspect that a certain sign of abnormality in the nervous system is present, but will require the highly specialised assurance of the neurologist in coming to a firm conclusion. If the paediatrician has not asked for an EEG the neurologist will himself request one, and at this point a few children previously thought to be autistic may be shown to have abnormalities in the brain structure which account for their slowness, i.e. their subnormality and also their limited or non-existent speech. The neurologist may be instrumental, therefore, in diagnosing those children suffering from organic brain damage whose problems are in no way linked with autism. If indeed there are organic factors then a little of the parents' possible feelings of guilt may be assuaged by explanations from the neurologist that difficulties could derive from an organic background. It is important to remember that the suspected presence of organic factors serves to exclude a diagnosis of autism in the classical sense. In cases where the neurologist finds no physical abnormality in the nervous system the diagnosis of autism becomes more probable and the need for the placement at a unit for purposes of more accurate diagnosis is strongly indicated.

Should a patient arrive at a neurological clinic having had no paediatric assessment or allied tests then the neurologist must investigate the case from the beginning, arranging the EEG readings, audiometry and possibly psychological assessment before he can make a diagnosis. It is likely that he would refer the child to the paediatrician at some point if he had never seen this consultant. There are cases where a dual diagnosis has to be considered, for example when a child has sustained a head injury but, nevertheless, on clinical grounds presents a case of autism. Under such circumstances several visits to the neurologist may be necessary and, of course, in certain cases already placed in a special school for diagnostic purposes, regular periodic neurological assessments may be requested by the consultant psychiatrist who visits the centre.

5 The consultant in electroencephalography

This doctor is in the unusual position that, in making assessments relating to the clinical state of the child's nervous system, he may never see the child. His basic role is to offer his interpretative skills, based on years of study of encephalography in relation to the recording of the child's brain waves as obtained by the encephalographer (or EEG recordist). Thus his function is almost completely diagnostic; though in a certain small proportion of cases whose brain wave patterns show a special area or 'focus' of abnormality he may feel that specific medication is indicated, thus helping in the treatment programme. This nearly always happens when in the process of interpretation, the EEG consultant can confirm a diagnosis of organic damage in the brain tissue which appears to be associated with subnormality and thereby virtually excluding the likelihood of autism. Clearly in cases that have been firmly diagnosed as autistic, the EEG consultant's expertise may not be called on again. However, the situation is open-ended and a psychiatrist, psychologist or paediatrician may at any time ask for a repeat EEG to be reported on. It is not an uncommon experience that a child who exhibited no abnormality on a first recording does so at the second, third or fourth attempt. When in doubt, any of the EEG consultant's colleagues may return to him for further diagnostic help with a puzzling case.

Where a first recording is unsatisfactory, due to the child's erratic behaviour during the recording session, it is normal practice for the EEG consultant to request a sleep recording. The child is given appropriate sedation before recording starts; the result then obtained may show much more significant patterns.

6 The audiologist

The advice of the audiologist may have been sought even earlier than that of the paediatrician. This would inevitably be so if the question of the child's hearing capacity is in doubt. The most significant factors that would make parents and doctors suspect that the child had a partial or complete hearing loss would be the lack of verbal or non-verbal response and the fact that normal speech was not developing. It is not easy to obtain a true assessment of the hearing ability of an autistic child. Initially such children may be too distressed in the test situation to allow the earphones to be placed on their heads. Nevertheless, the possibility that deafness is the true cause for what appear to be 'autistic' characteristics must always be considered and if possible excluded. Deafness may well be a significant causative feature in the differential diagnosis of autism. For this reason repeated attempts at assessment must be made at regular intervals. It is usually found that after a time the child becomes sufficiently familiarised with the audiologist

171

and his equipment for a hearing record (audiogram) to be made. One test alone is not sufficient and it is only when there is consistency of findings over a period of repeated investigations that a true assessment is thought to have been arrived at. Even at this point further tests are necessary to confirm that there has been no clinical distortion, for it has been shown that there can be an apparent and measurable functional hearing loss at times of extreme emotion. The hearing (or listening) ability of autistic children seems to decrease with high emotional stress, and, although this is to a certain extent true for everyone, there is evidence that it is particularly so in autism.

7   The speech therapist

In a sense the speech therapist takes over when the audiologist leaves off, for when the assessment of hearing has been made the speech therapist must build on what speech there is or, if none exists, prepare the child in various ways for speech to emerge. These would include breathing exercises and repetitive buccal movements. The speech therapist may be more involved in the day-to-day development of the child's progress than any other specialist apart from the teacher. There is therefore a great need, in those centres fortunate enough to have speech therapy provision, for sympathetic understanding and warm co-operation between teacher and speech therapist in relation to each individual child. The speech therapist is regarded as an indispensable member of the team within the special school or unit and one who, in terms of her own expertise, can assess the child's progress. She will want to comment on and compare the child's developing speech patterns with the teachers and, from time to time, talk to the child's parents either alone or in company with the Head of the school and the teacher involved. There is thus a very necessary overlap between the role of the speech therapist and the teacher, the former interpreting more specific progress in speech, while the latter relates this to the child's global development.

8   The ear, nose and throat surgeon

The surgeon specialising in the diseases of the ear, nose and

throat is frequently asked by one of the other medical specialists to examine a child who has an apparent hearing loss. In
most instances an audiogram has already been carried out,
but a negative result in such a test does not necessarily exclude
the possibility of a hearing loss being present. The practical
difficulties of the procedure in disturbed children have already
been discussed. Diagnostically it is extremely useful if the ENT
surgeon can exclude beyond doubt the existence of a pathological condition likely to produce a partial hearing loss. This
opinion may serve to confirm the diagnosis of autism where
doubt has existed previously, and the teachers and others concerned with the child can then approach the problem with
increased confidence.

9 The dental surgeon

In general terms the role of the dentist with regard to the
autistic child is essentially the same as it is with his other
patients. Nevertheless his task is an extremely difficult one and
one that some dentists do not feel that they can undertake.
Many autistic children resist to an extreme degree all attempts
even to inspect their teeth. It is not unknown for the dentist to
be bitten and his equipment scattered. One solution has been
to do all essential treatment with the child under sedation, but
there are difficulties in this for it cannot be done in the
ordinary dental clinics and special hospital centres, where
such treatment can be given, are few in number. Some dentists
accept the co-operation of a teacher or other person who can
manage to control the child's behaviour sufficiently for him to
carry out the treatment, but this does require a high degree of
tact and tolerance on the part of both. Nevertheless, it is
important that the children have proper dental care and
recently training has begun to acquaint dentists with the problems involved and techniques for coping with the children's extremely resistant behaviour. These do involve the dentist
having to spend much more time on each patient than is commonly practicable; it may for instance take several sessions to
get the child willing to co-operate before treatment can begin.
A dentist who is prepared to attempt to treat autistic children
may occasionally find himself in the role of a diagnostician in,

for example, the case of a young child who is brought in for treatment by parents who have not, to that time, sought any medical advice for their child. His training and experience will enable him to detect how abnormal the child's behaviour is, and in talking to the mother about the child's early history in relation to speech and development he is likely to elicit a few relevant facts including the name of the GP who may, in some circumstances, never have seen the child. Having suggested to the parents the wisdom of seeking the advice and opinion of the doctor, the dentist can contact the GP (having told the parents he intended to do so) and alert him to the fact that the child's symptoms require further investigation. If he feels it to be appropriate he can also tell the doctor that the parents may be apprehensive and resistant to medical help.

10 The social worker

Social workers are normally part of a psychiatric team, the other essential members of which are the psychiatrist and the psychologist. The team is generally based on either a hospital, or child guidance centre. The social worker is mainly concerned with the family, and a great part of her time is spent on visiting the family at home. This enables her to become familiar with the home and all the members of the family, and in so doing to gain insight into the whole situation. At the same time it allows the family to get to know her in such a way that she can become their adviser and friend. She also acts as the essential link and channel of communication between the parents and other members of the team, who normally are more directly involved with the child who is their patient.

The social worker's part in helping the family can only begin after a child has been referred to a psychiatrist as being in need of investigation and possibly treatment. This can happen when the child is very young and a health visitor is still visiting the house advising and supporting the family. In this case it is a matter of tactfully co-operating and dove-tailing the services so that the parents do not appear to have to choose whose advice they wish to follow. Normally it is the case that the health visitor gradually withdraws and 'hands over' to the social worker, for the social worker has an important role for as long as the child remains a patient of the psychiatrist.

Sometimes this role continues even after the child has been placed in a special school. In some instances the school is part of the social worker's field of work, and in these cases the social worker acts as interpreter and channel of information between the school and the teachers, and the parents and the home, in the same way as she functions in the clinic. There are some advantages in this arrangement particularly if the same psychiatrist visits both the school and the clinic from which the social worker operates. There are, however, practical and other reasons why this is not always the best plan, and in these instances the social worker tends to withdraw from active involvement with the family after the child has settled in the school. She would resume her active role if the child had to remain a patient of the psychiatrist after he had left the school.

11   The educational psychologist

The psychologist has studied in depth the functioning of man's mind in health and in disease both during the developmental years and in maturity. He has learnt to assess ability levels quantitatively in each age group and to relate them to realistic expectations of achievement. His skills enable him to interpret how variations of behaviour may modify or inhibit basic ability and to recognise special cases as, for instance, where the potential intelligence is very low.

Educational and clinical psychologists are frequently asked to make assessment, using psychological tests, of children considered to be autistic, as part of the process of differential diagnosis. A child with apparently no understanding of language or much comprehension of his environment may reveal such abilities when tested. The Reynell test of language development, for instance, examines the child's receptive understanding as well as his ability in oral expression. The administration of this test to an autistic child may well demonstrate that, although the child cannot use language for speech, he can respond appropriately to such a command as, 'Put the penny under the cup.' Correct and incorrect responses to similar tasks will then produce a 'receptive language age' which can be compared to that of other children.

Intelligence tests are often administered to obtain information about both general level of functioning (IQ) and abilities in specific tasks. While the IQ obtained may be in the subnormal range, a child's ability on some tasks may reveal areas of normal or above average functioning. The pattern of scores he produces may give important clues for teaching strategies.

It has been noted previously how difficult it can be to obtain rapport with an autistic child. Often the psychologist is faced with a child who is untestable because he will not respond. When this happens the psychologist has to use other methods of appraising the child's potential, and this may best be done in his home environment by careful observation. Here the child may give evidence of cognitive potential in the way he handles familiar domestic objects or play materials such as his own jigsaws and constructional toys. By his knowledge of the norms of a child's development the psychologist will be able to assess which activities are significantly retarded or within the normal or above average range of ability.

The psychologist may also play a part in the treatment programme. The knowledge of the child he has gained from testing and from observation can be of use to teachers when arranging learning objectives and strategies for dealing with the child's behaviour. Lastly an educational psychologist can be useful in arranging a suitable school placement when it is considered that transfer to a more normal environment is necessary. Sometimes such a transfer is not easy to arrange. The child will have made good progress in some areas, say speech and academic subjects, while in others, for instance social awareness, he may still be lacking. In this case a careful appraisal will need to be made in the matching of child and school. The educational psychologist will have good knowledge of the schools in his area and if he knows the child's abilities and disabilities he will probably be the best person to evaluate the possibilities. What he will look for is a school that can cope not only with the child's residual problems but one which can also build on the progress already established. Schools differ in the ways in which they are organised and the teaching methods they employ, and these factors may be significant aspects to be taken into account when providing for the handicapped child's special needs.

12 The psychiatrist

The psychiatrist has a dual role to fulfil with regard to autistic children and their parents. He has in the first place to take a great part in diagnosis and, second, he is responsible for deciding and initiating treatment. This will probably include giving advice on the most suitable form of schooling even though the psychologist is responsible for collating the various specialist opinions in this respect and passing them on to the local authority. Frequently the psychiatrist's most important task begins after the diagnostic procedures are completed and consists of giving support to the parents at every stage of the child's history. If the psychiatrist is acting as consultant to a special school then he has also the task of advising on and at times interpreting to the teachers aspects of the behaviour of both the children and the parents and their own reactions to it.

The psychiatrist and the parents

Only those who have been intimately connected with children coming within the diagnostic category of autism are able to realise fully the complexities of guilt, hostility, anxiety and depression which their parents suffer. Sometimes they feel entirely alone in their trouble for the father and mother may not be able to communicate with each other on this, the most stressful problem that they share. The psychiatrist can help them to deal with this even if only to the extent of helping them to realise the true problem. The following case histories will illustrate.

Linda was 3 years and 3 months old when she was referred to the psychiatrist by a doctor at the welfare clinic because she was restless, 'lived in a world of her own', and her mother had no control over her. Linda proved to be seriously retarded with little or no speech, her mother remarking that, 'Linda does not seem to regard speech as a necessary means of communication.'

Further contact with the family revealed that the mother had been 'tired' during the pregnancy, suffering from psoriasis throughout. As a young baby Linda was slow to feed and cried constantly; as she grew older she showed no affection and did not relate to adults. In a separate interview Linda's father showed a severely depressed pattern of thinking (prior to his marriage he had planned the date and place of his own suicide). He was so deeply guilt-ridden that he, together with his wife, regarded Linda's arrival as a just retribution for their 'sins'. She was a punishment with which they must continually live, and when placement at an in-patient unit for assessment was suggested for Linda after her state had worsened, for she had started biting both dogs and people, it was refused for it was they, the parents, who could not separate from, or survive, without Linda.

Some parents are deeply depressed when they try to come to terms with both the difficult behaviour of the child and their fears for his future. One mother was already failing to meet the demands of her eldest son Hugh, then $4\frac{1}{2}$ years old, and of the rest of the family, when her GP sent her to a child guidance clinic for advice. Hugh was a nice-looking, chubby-faced, golden-haired boy who literally ran round his mother in circles, pulling at her clothes and shouting and jumping. When he noticed the thick flex leading to the telephone he became absorbed in that for about a quarter of an hour, after which he began to run between that and the light switch. His mother commented that plugs were his 'chief delight' at that time. Hugh began to spit on and lick the telephone muttering a coherent phrase, 'Daddy mend it.' His mother reported that at 18 months he was obsessed with banging doors, opening and shutting them perpetually. As a baby he showed no affection and was apparently unaware of people until about the age of 3. Then he suddenly started to relate to people in a quite undiscriminating way, cuddling anyone who arrived at the house, whether it was an aunt or a postman.

Hugh's mother was so exhausted by his restlessness at night as well as by day, that from time to time a relative took care of the new baby (then 6 months old) to give her some rest. Her life had been made even more difficult as her middle child had started to behave with the same restlessness as Hugh. Not surprisingly, this young mother had become distraught and depressed, and experienced great relief when Hugh was admitted to an observation unit. Hugh's story to date is a happy one, for, within a year of his admission to an in-patient unit for non-communicating children, he was able to return home and to attend the local school. Although he was a 'loner' in the school situation, he nevertheless settled and proved to be quite a bright child. The younger brother (the middle child), however, continued to follow Hugh's pattern and in time had to be admitted to the same in-patient unit.

Hugh's parents gladly accepted and followed the advice they were offered. There are other parents who, although they appear to be able to accept the diagnosis and the need for special placement, are seemingly confused and inclined to be rigid. They nod wisely but find it difficult to put into practice the advice they have been given and apparently accepted. In these cases, the psychiatrist must play a continuing role, supporting the parents in their reluctant agreement at every stage. This is where the help of the social worker is particularly valuable. The therapeutic role of the psychiatrist in relation to the parents of the autistic children in his care is inevitably affected by the specific parental attitudes developed during the pre-diagnostic and post-diagnostic period. The longer the time the different specialists take in coming to a decision about the child's basic condition the more confused, anxious and disturbed the parents may become. Happily the converse can also be true since a slower pace taken in diagnosis can allow time for parental adjustment.

It would not be surprising if a proportion of parents actively rejected their abnormal children but this attitude is not so frequently encountered as that of ambivalence, which often shows in undue concern and over-protectiveness. The parents of children exhibiting any form of handicap frequently have to cope with their own anxiety and 'guilt feeling' as to whether they are responsible for their child's problem. This is particularly likely to be the case when, as with autism, nobody as yet can specifically state the cause of the handicap. In consequence mothers especially are prone to relate the child's clinical state to such things as their own feelings of rejection of him at some stage either at the time of conception or perhaps later during the post-natal and infant feeding stage. For example, if breast feeding had been attempted and proved difficult, the mother might recall her acute despair through what would

179

have seemed endless nights with a perpetually crying baby. Maternal depression is well recognised as a clinical entity at these times and frequently feelings of guilt form part of the symptomatology. Recalling the time when she had overtly rejected her child and resented nursing him the mother might feel that this past emotion had promoted the child's condition. In such cases it is the task of the psychiatrist to help the mother to 'work through' this guilt.

A residual and unhappy duty will fall to the lot of the psychiatrist if it becomes established that a child formerly considered as a possible case of autism, has an irrefutable diagnosis of subnormality confirmed, and that is to bring the parents to the point of acceptance as painlessly as possible and to offer support when it is concluded that the child's condition is not going to be significantly changed by the treatment.

The psychiatrist as consultant adviser in a school

The psychiatrist working as consultant adviser in a special school has several roles to play. First, he is involved, with the Headteacher and the referring specialists, in the selection of the children to be admitted to the school. Similarly, he is consulted when the decision is taken that a child is ready to leave that school and move to another. Second, he is concerned with helping and supporting the parents of the children attending the school in the ways illustrated above. Third, he has a therapeutic responsibility for the children, some of whom he may see individually; the amount of time he can spend on this is largely determined by the number of sessions he can spend at the school. And fourth, he can act as an expert adviser to the teachers, contributing to their greater understanding of the children in their care by interpreting to them some of the possible motivations and emotions which lead the children, the parents and perhaps themselves to act and react in the ways that they do. This is commonly done by holding staff conferences or may occasionally take the form of private discussions with individual members of the staff. An example of the kind of topic which could be discussed in either of these ways, apart from the obvious questions arising from the children's behaviour, would be the ambivalent feelings towards the staff which are sometimes displayed by the parents. Here the psychiatrist could point out that the teacher's success with a child might, in the parents' view, underline their feelings of guilt, failure and inadequacy. An appreciation of this could help the teacher who might otherwise feel surprised and unhappy that the parents do not appear to value what he is attempting to do for their child. Similarly to a teacher without any experience of working with autistic children the methods of teaching that have to be employed at times might appear strange, even harsh, at the beginning. At this time, the teacher will benefit from the opportunity to talk about the child's reactions, his day-to-day behaviour and his interaction in the group, and it is valuable if he has available a psychiatric, as well as an educational interpretation of his observations. This again would be a topic for discussion in a staff conference at which ideally the psychologist and speech therapist were also present.

Conclusion

In this chapter the roles of the many specialists who may be involved both in the diagnosis and treatment of autistic children have been described. Obviously the services of them all are not required in every case, and the degree to which they are easily available varies considerably throughout the country. What is important is that such services as are essential are known and easily available to the parents and those attempting to help them and their children.

9   Summary and discussion

BARBARA FURNEAUX AND
BRIAN ROBERTS

In this book we have attempted to survey and discuss the topic of autism and the many problems it imposes on the children suffering from this severe handicap, their parents and families, the people who are involved in advising and teaching them, and those who are responsible for setting up suitable provision to meet their needs.

Although the condition was first recognised and described by Leo Kanner in 1943 there are still many unresolved questions as, for example, the aetiology of the syndrome. The current hypotheses in this respect have been considered in chapter 2 of this book. At present it is open to question whether one can correctly discuss a syndrome of autism, for the term is used in many different ways and covers all children displaying the associated symptoms from a mild to a severe degree. Originally the term was only used when the 'autistic' features were present but there was no detectable evidence of organic or neurological damage. This is no longer invariably the case, for it is now sometimes used to describe all children showing certain behavioural and language disorders regardless of whether they are organically or otherwise damaged. The consequences of this confused use of the term have been discussed in several of our chapters. Until there is an agreed definition it is extremely difficult to compare and evaluate research findings and different therapeutic and educational approaches. In the present circumstances in all written or spoken discussions of the topic it would seem to be essential to state as exactly as possible the condition of the children to whom the discussion applies.

The problems of differential diagnosis are dealt with in chapters 2 and 3. Here it only needs to be recalled that the

182

groups we are referring to are those children who are known to have no accompanying disabling condition such as deafness, partial-sightedness or neurological damage and who do exhibit the major features of autism.

Age and provision for autistic children

The question of when to begin teaching treatment with autistic children relates to two issues: (1) the age at which a firm diagnosis of the condition can be made, and (2) the local educational authority's policy on age of school entry. The normal policy in England and Wales is for the child to start school at the beginning of the term in which he will attain the age of 5. There are a number of difficulties in diagnosis (see chapters 2 and 3), one of which is that the diagnostician may adopt a 'wait and see' policy, on the basis that a cautious unwillingness to 'label' the child prematurely will be in the family's and the child's best interests. This is, of course, a difficult decision which involves implicit problems. If the child has to wait for normal school entry age for admission to a specialised unit much valuable time may have been lost in dealing with the remediation of his problems. On the other hand some children exhibiting delay in speech or other abilities may go on to develop quite normally, as late as their third, or even their fourth year in a few cases.

It is reasonable to expect by the third birthday that the child has shown development in terms of relating to adults, siblings and peers, that he will be able to follow some instructions, and that he will have developed some speech. Where these skills are not in evidence and there are some accompanying autistic traits, then it is at this age that specialised teaching should be arranged for most of the children. It may be that with a small number of these children there remains some uncertainty as to the presence or otherwise of symptoms which appear to implicate neurological dysfunction or damage, but it is wise to consider including these also. From age 3 on all the children should be regularly re-appraised, especially in view of the findings illustrated in chapter 3 on differential diagnosis.

The earlier treatment begins the sooner successes may be expected. This is true, perhaps, in the treatment of all kinds of behaviour problems where behaviour may become increasingly intransigent when special help is not sought, or is not available. However, given the severity of the problems of autistic children, and the repercussions on the family and all who come in contact with them, it can be seen that some, at least, of the severely disordered behaviour may itself be a reflection of the inability of the adults in the child's environment to cope.

The beginnings of a school programme to deal with the behaviour should, as pointed out in chapter 4, be accompanied, where possible, by a structured home programme. This twin attack on the child's and family's problem will help to ensure that the parents gain a sense of optimism which may aid in alleviating the great strains which the family endures. As active partners in the treatment of their child they may well come to feel that they can cope in what was beginning to seem a hopeless cause.

The question arises, what provision is there for such children beginning at the age of 3? There is probably provision in most, if not all, local education authorities for the blind, deaf, partially sighted and partially hearing children to begin schooling from the age of 2. Officially, specific provision for autistic children was not regarded as necessary until 1972, and it is unlikely in view of recent financial cuts in education that many authorities have initiated early provision for these children as yet. There is a need therefore for those diagnosing the condition to argue the importance of provision being made at the age of 3, for the problems involved are at least as pressing as those involving deafness and blindness.

Further it must perhaps also be argued that in centres of dense population where there are likely to be a number of diagnosed autistic children there should be a clear policy on how the provision should be made, whether in classes in special schools or in ordinary schools or in separate special schools or units. In rural areas there will be additional problems since it is unlikely that there will be sufficient cases to make local provision practicable. Transport will therefore be necessary to take the children to areas where special help has been organised.

184

Integration of the treated child into other schools

Where such early provision is available, it is to be hoped that some of the children will be able to move into normal schools or those for the educationally subnormal at late infant or middle school age, i.e. between age 6 at the very earliest or at the latest by the age of 11, since in many areas this is still the age of transfer to secondary or comprehensive education.

There are two main views about the criteria to be used in deciding that the time has come to transfer the child to a normal school, and a further deciding factor will be the type of provision which is available in the area. Some teachers of autistic children believe that before integration is attempted a child should have competence in academic skills, language and social skills at about the same level as those children with whom he will spend his time in school. Others feel that when some progress has been shown in these areas, attempts at integration should begin. If this plan is followed the child is integrated over a long period of time; he will go first with a teacher from his special school or unit to the normal school for playtimes, and perhaps lunch-time, gym, music and movement periods, etc. Then with the co-operation of the class teacher of the new school the child will begin part-time schooling with the special teacher remaining with him in the class. This serves several purposes; she is on call to deal with any difficulties which arise, and she can aid the integration with the other children in social situations e.g. working together on a project. Gradually, however, she withdraws and the class teacher takes over.

This strategy has its advantages and its drawbacks. To make it possible the special school needs a very high teacher/child ratio. It also requires a great deal of co-operation from the new school and patently the staff will need to be sympathetic to this type of child. The Head, class teacher and all the other adults coming into contact with the child will need to be fully informed as to all the possible consequences of this gradual integration of the child into the school. Practically it will also be far more convenient if the two schools and the child's home are not too far apart. This is particularly important in the case

185

of the home and the new school, so that any relationships with his peers that the child builds up in school can be developed further outside school hours.

There are strong arguments for and against this plan even if the essential conditions mentioned above can be met, and this will certainly not always be the case. On the positive side it is possible that the earlier association with normal children it ensures may accelerate the child's rate of progress, especially in social terms, because he will have normal models to imitate and ultimately identify with. It may also mean that the special school can deal with a larger number of children since there should be a faster turnover than if the alternative scheme is followed. On the negative side, it can result in the children being marked out from the start as different from the other children in the normal school, and this could have long-term consequences in determining the attitudes and expectations of the teachers and the other children. It also means that the special school or unit will be dealing always in the main with those children with the severest difficulties; hence it will lack 'models' for the children and the teachers will get little reinforcement for themselves in terms of 'feedback'. The probability is that the case of each child who seems likely to benefit from the early type of integration will need to be separately evaluated in the light of all these points.

Some children will not have made sufficient progress to enter normal or ESN school until secondary school stage and this may involve greater problems. Even the transfer of normal children at this stage can cause difficulties because of the size and complexity of organisation of these schools; for instance the child will no longer have one teacher but may have to adapt to as many as nine or ten as he moves from one subject to another. Fortunately most secondary schools have remedial provision (although the amount and quality of this provision may be very variable) in which small numbers of pupils do work mainly with one teacher, and these special classes may be able to help the child initially, and so ease his integration into the normal classes if and when he is ready to cope with them. A few secondary schools in most local authorities have units for 'delicate' children (a term which covers a large variety of medical and behavioural conditions) and the treated autistic

186

child is often well catered for in such a unit. Again some local authorities as for example the Inner London Education Authority which has opened a special school near Wimbledon Common, and Surrey County Council which is making provision in the Linden Bridge School, are now filling a previously serious gap by catering for the needs of the older autistic children who still need specific educational treatment.

The need for continuing educational treatment

There is a growing body of evidence that autistic children, and indeed other handicapped children, can go on improving if their education can be continued beyond the normal school leaving age. On the whole this applies to the less able of the children since the others will have moved on to ordinary schools and their education will follow the normal course; but there will also be a few with delayed potential who for one reason or another (e.g. a late entry into the special school) have not been able to transfer. There is therefore a growing demand that continuing provision should be made and that it should be the responsibility of the education authorities. The National Society for Autistic Children is pioneering in this field and is beginning to open establishments for this purpose. Sybil Elgar in chapter 6 describes the work she is doing in what was the first of these, Somerset Court. In the relatively short time that it has been open she is able to report improvement for some of the young people, and that there has been no deterioration in the condition of the least able. This is a far more positive statement than it appears to be on first impression. At Somerset Court, the younger residents are the charge of their local education authorities, and the older ones (age 18 and over) of the social services. They are all considered to be in an educational situation.

Although it will probably be generally accepted that it is totally correct to stress the need to make continuing educational provision during the time that it can be demonstrated that improvements are taking place, it cannot be denied that this provision is very expensive. In a time of economic stringency, and where there are competing claims for the limited funds which are available, it may be necessary to

187

decide that evaluation according to agreed criteria is essential, and a limit set to the length of time for which this provision can be made if improvement does not take place. There is a further problem in that there is a danger that the population in such establishments may become fixed and that what started as an educational institution may become, in the course of time, a geriatric home. It will become increasingly difficult to make the decision to move a person from a place to which he has become accustomed, especially if the place to which he is to be moved is, outwardly at least, far less attractive. Nevertheless, these are issues that may have to be faced.

Teacher–child ratio

In the severest state of his condition, the autistic child's behaviour will necessitate virtually one-to-one handling. Probably few local education authorities allow for such high teacher ratios. The circular about autistic children issued by the Department of Education and Science suggested as a guideline, one adult (this includes teachers and teacher's assistants) to deal with three children. It can be seen that in a class of, say, six children with a teacher and assistant, no child could receive more than 50 per cent of the time on a one-to-one basis without detriment to the other five. However, if the ratio is increased to one-to-one, then it becomes possible to give all the children this amount of individual attention, for while one child is receiving it the others can be engaged in activities which do not require such close supervision. The point is that one-to-three provision is expensive in the first place, but will not be cost-effective if it does not deal satisfactorily with the problem. If however, one extra adult were to be supplied the immediate cost would increase but expense should be saved in the long run if it resulted in effective work being done which led to the child's being able to transfer to other educational provision relatively quickly. It seems possible that the higher the teacher ratio initially the greater may be the overall financial saving.

Social behaviour of near-normal autistic children and adolescents

When an autistic child has reached the stage where he can converse reasonably well and understand other people, and can cope with academic and other work at at least a satisfactory level (some achieve far more than this), there are often residual problems, mainly in the social skills. During a child's acutely autistic phase the normal experiences of childhood and of social exchanges and relationships have passed unobserved and unheeded. In consequence he literally does not know how to relate appropriately to other people, either peers or adults, nor what are the accepted codes of behaviour. A normal child in the course of growing up learns how to relate by observation, by experience, and by 'trial and error', in addition to being told how to respond to others. Consequently, relating is not merely a mechanical activity practised according to rules. The recovering autistic child, however, very often has to learn the rules in a pedantic fashion. A frequent feature of these children is that they ask many questions about the intentions of others as do young children who ask, 'Why does he do that . . . say that', etc. Often they seem unable to grasp, or to be unaware of, what the behaviour of others signifies. Similarly they are unable to monitor or assess their own behaviour in terms of how it appears to other people. This can lead to their company being avoided by their peers who can be either embarrassed or bored if, for example, they find themselves having to listen to a long and detailed monologue about something they were only superficially interested in, in the first place. This, unfortunately, can happen frequently, for the 'recovered' autistic child has the tendency to talk at great length on a topic which interests him and is unable to pick up the cues that would signify to a normal person that his audience does not share his interest.

When normal adults are in, or put into, unusual situations (as has been done in experiments in social psychology) — ones that are perceived as unstructured or structured in a novel way — they either seek information about the position they should take, or attempt to withdraw. Often the required

189

information is, or has to be, sought in a discreet, roundabout way. To the child who has been autistic, most situations will be novel as he emerges from his isolation, and it is his task to try to discover, or to decipher, what is happening; his alternative is to avoid the event, which is the less daunting and therefore more tempting, thing to do. This in itself can be seen as autistic behaviour to those who are ignorant of what the child's or adolescent's problems are.

This has important repercussions, especially at the time when such children are beginning to take a sexual interest in the opposite sex, for here their social immaturity and lack of experience puts them at a great disadvantage. They do not know how to make or interpret the initial advances; for example, they tend to overreact to a show of friendship frequently to such a degree that the other person withdraws, and they feel puzzled, and hurt by, what seems to them to be an unmerited rebuff. Their normal tendency to interpret statements with complete literalness can also lead to difficult or dangerous situations, as for example happened to a girl who was nearly exploited by a man who was a casual acquaintance. She trustingly accepted his statement that 'every girl had to be taught how to have sex', followed by the offer, and attempt, to be her teacher! It follows from this that social situations will have to be facilitated for these young people by adults who realise the nature of their difficulties in these situations. This is an important aspect of their further education. Where they do not ask, they must be given adequate information or demonstration of what is required, in the understanding that they are simply and literally ignorant of this. Their questions will need sympathetic and patient response for they will often appear quite inappropriate to their age. *For they will appear odd when the oddity is quite simply ignorance.* The result of course is that they may be shunned by those of their own age and even by adults, and this can have a very deleterious effect on a progress which to that point has been very encouraging. Where the child is young enough still to be in school and living at home, the task of giving him this social education will properly fall upon his parents, family and teachers. It may well be that, at present, it is not started at an early enough age. This is not surprising in view of multiplicity of other problems that have

190

to be dealt with. Nevertheless, if the need is fully appreciated, it can be built in to the day-to-day programme and management and, hopefully, this will help to ensure that the child is not so totally lacking in social experiences as he commonly is at present. Hence he will not be at such a great disadvantage as he gets older. The problem of continuing to supply the help needed as the child moves out into normal society has often neither been recognised nor fully resolved yet, partly because it is only now that more of the 'treated' children are coming to a stage where the need is being fully displayed and appreciated. The aid of such people as Youth Employment Officers, Colleges of Further Education, Church and other youth club leaders and organisers will have to be enlisted.

For many young people the transfer to adult working and social life can be difficult; for the ex-autistic child it can be a very tenuous and stressful event, and it needs to be graded and structured in a way that allows the young person to make increasingly better sense of it. There are bound to be unfortunate 'accidents' along the way, but the more the people in the environments the child encounters are alerted to the kind of pitfalls that may arise, the more promising the child's progress is likely to be. He has a great deal to learn about the world and, in making up for literally lost time, the autistic child's development may not appear to have reached maturity in social terms until he has reached his late teens or twenties. Some may never achieve it.

The need for continuing research

In chapter 7 a number of current research findings have been discussed and critically examined. Their relevance to the teacher in the classroom has been indicated and also the practical applications of the findings. There is still a great deal to be discovered and established both about the causes of the condition, the children who can correctly be considered as belonging to this diagnostic category, and the best techniques for helping them—hence there is a continuing need for medical, psychological and educational research. On the medical side it is hoped that more bio-chemical investigations will be carried out, for there are some observed features and

191

abnormalities in the children which indicate that such research might reveal some highly relevant information. Since it is generally agreed that the lack of ability to communicate is a very important handicapping feature, and since some of the children never achieve speech while others do so painfully slowly and in a very limited way, research into such children's ability to acquire alternative methods of communication would obviously be desirable, in spite of the fact that they would only have limited practical application. It may be necessary to set up a residential centre for the purpose, since there are practical difficulties in properly applying such a system as, for example, the Paget-Gorman sign language in a day school. These difficulties would not be insuperable, however, if the positive value of the system to this group of children had been positively established. These are just two examples of what still remains to be investigated.

Conclusion

It has recently been calculated (personal communication, Lorna Wing, 1976) that there are approximately 5,000 autistic children in England and Wales, about half of whom are typical cases while the rest have many of the symptoms. It is claimed that the handicap has such specific features that the children suffering from it need specialised teaching to a degree comparable to that with visually and aurally handicapped children. There are slightly more autistic children than there are blind and partially sighted children and slightly less than the number of deaf children.

Nevertheless there is by no means such adequate provision made for their educational needs. Education cannot 'cure' the autistic child any more than it can cure the blind child. It has been shown, though, that given the education appropriate to their needs, some of them are capable of living an independent life within the community, while others can become contributing members in a sheltered community. In purely practical terms the cost of educating both of these groups has been justified, since without it they would have been a charge to the community for the whole of their lives. There is a need therefore for:

more diagnostic facilities;
more resources for family support and relief;
more schools;
much more provision for the adolescent and young adult;
more facilities for after-care and support;
more research.
All of these things cost money but they do give a chance of normal life to children who without help would remain cut off and withdrawn, prisoners within what has been called their 'empty fortress'. Can we, as a caring community afford not to provide them?